Anne Hooper's

Sexual
Intimacy

Anne Hooper's
Sexual
Intimacy

DORLING KINDERSLEY

LONDON ▪ NEW YORK ▪ STUTTGART ▪ MOSCOW

A DK PUBLISHING BOOK

Created and produced by
CARROLL & BROWN LIMITED
5 Lonsdale Road
London NW6 6RA

Publishing Director Denis Kennedy
Art Director Chrissie Lloyd

Project Editors Ian Wood, Laura Price
Art Editor Paul Stradling

Photographer Alistair Hughes

Production Wendy Rogers, Kate Disney

First American Edition, 1996
2 4 6 8 10 9 7 5 3 1

Published in the United States by DK Publishing, Inc.
95 Madison Avenue, New York, New York 10016
Visit us on the World Wide Web at http://www.dk.com

Library of Congress Cataloging-in-Publication Data
Hooper, Anne
    Anne Hooper's Sexual intimacy. – – 1st American ed.
        p.   cm.
    Includes bibliographical references and index.
    ISBN 0-7894-1059-1
    1. Sex.   2. Intimacy (Psychology) 3. Man-woman relationships.
    I.   Title.
    HQ31.H735 1996
    613.9'6– –dc20   96–5536
                                                      CIP

Reproduced by Colourscan, Singapore
Printed in Italy by New Interlitho S.p.A. - Milan

FOREWORD

I've noticed, over the past ten years, that the men and women coming to me for counseling have been increasingly concerned with the quality of their relationships. Sex is very important, they agree, but so too is that indefinable something, that air between them that all is well and feeling satisfactory. These people are talking about the quality of intimacy.

What all of them have in common is puzzlement when I explain that intimacy isn't really about sex, even though it may profoundly affect sexual experience. Most people wrongly assume that intimacy is synonymous with sex. It's not. It's as much about emotions as it is about sex, because your ability to be "good at intimacy" relates directly to the person you believe you are, your "self."

It's those "selves" (formed mainly in childhood, but now inside the shells of adults) who show up in my office. The problem is often that one partner's idea of intimacy doesn't match with that of the other partner. And my job, as a therapist, is to find ways for each to interpret the other's intimacy. This can be exciting. Strong men and women may cry. But they are sharing emotions and developing new feelings of tenderness and sympathy as a result. At the very least, I hope they emerge with a greater understanding of who they are. As I hope you do after reading this book.

Anne Hooper

CONTENTS

INTRODUCTION

Intimacy is what most people look for in marriage or any other type of long-term loving relationship, and it is one of the things they miss most when a relationship ends. Virtually all lovers agree that sexuality is a vital ingredient of keeping tenderness alive.

Sexual intimacy forms an important part of the long-term intimacy needed in any marriage, and its loss often triggers a type of marital erosion. When this occurs, it can be terribly difficult for you to regain the degree of intimacy you may once have felt for your partner, even if your marriage appears to have been stable and strong for years.

If the sex doesn't work very well, there is sadly, almost inevitably, a withdrawal of love and trust. These two, love and trust, are therefore the major ingredients needed to ensure and maintain sexual intimacy within a relationship.

Good sex – that which provides mutual pleasure and (hopefully) orgasms – is therefore very important. But what about the other sides of intimacy that relate directly to how sex is experienced? How the relationship functions as a whole has its bearing on how you approach each other between the sheets. And your relationship will rely on the degree of compatibility there is between you, and, just as important, how well you manage all those chunks of your life that are not so compatible.

EXAMINE YOUR BACKGROUND

Looking at where you and your partner come from is therefore of prime importance to your relationship. It is only by fully understanding your own background and that of your partner that you begin to see precisely how each of you has formulated your concept of "self." Your "self," that person who is you, is made up of attitudes, morality, views of the world, and personal imperatives that have been planted within you, primarily before the age of seven. And these views will depend on your birth order, those members of the family who had the most influence on you, and whether or not you understood, and drew realistic conclusions from, your early family teachings.

Once you gain insight into these factors you can plot a personal profile of your attitudes, and then take the next step, which is to compare your profile with that of your partner. In this way you obtain an understanding of the areas where you as a couple match and the areas where you differ.

SEX AND STABILITY
Marital breakdown occurs less frequently when partners are comfortable with sex and their own bodies.

Once this information is available, you possess valuable material with which to improve your skills of loving and being loved. With support and encouragement you can work on those areas where the differences cause problems.

IDENTIFYING YOUR SEXUAL INFLUENCES

As a sex therapist, I meet with many couples who complain of having a sex problem. Often, though, they can't tell me exactly what this consists of. They know that something is the matter, but they honestly can't identify just what it is. But if I breathe the magic word "intimacy," they jump on it. "That's it!" they cry. Somehow, they've mislaid intimacy.

So my first task is to try to establish why there isn't enough of this elusive quality. To do so, I determine what kind of climate exists. I manage this by asking my clients about the relationship between their mothers and their fathers. I encourage them to think about their parents, not just in terms of how happy or unhappy they were, but what their behavior showed. Did these parents touch each other? Did they hug, demonstrate love physically, tell one another "I love you"? The next questions are: "How did members of your family communicate with you? Were they loving in their tone of voice and actions? Did they shout when they were angry? Did they forbid the expression of anger? Were they punishing or encouraging?"

EXAMINING THE ANSWERS

Your answers to these basic queries add up to an emotional backdrop, a tapestry of what went on in your formative years, coloring all your expectations of any future close relationship. For you, the individual, this is what a relationship and a family consist of. In later life, provided you meet

up with a partner who has a broadly similar family background, everything will be fine. You will most likely find that the two of you are highly compatible, with an instinctive understanding of each other's behavior, able to make allowances where necessary and to show your love and support for one another.

The difficulties arise only when you and your partner have such different backgrounds that there is very little you can take for granted and therefore only a fraction of instinctive understanding. Thanks to your different backgrounds you develop different emotional expectations of

MUTUAL GIVING
Generosity with love can be shown in many ways, not least in simple pleasuring and grooming.

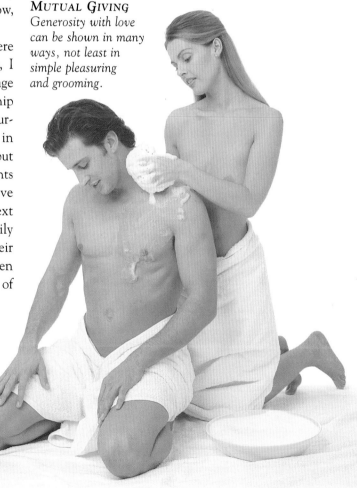

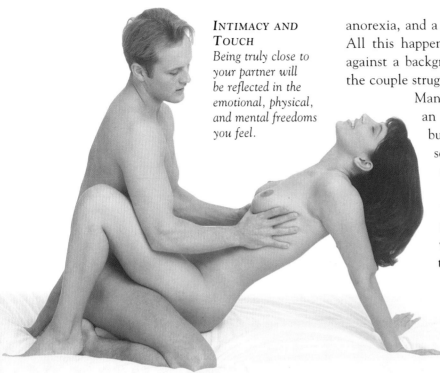

INTIMACY AND TOUCH
Being truly close to your partner will be reflected in the emotional, physical, and mental freedoms you feel.

anorexia, and a fire destroyed the family home. All this happened over the space of 15 years against a background of constant hard work as the couple struggled to get a business started.

Many marriages would have come to an end under such circumstances, but Edward and Mara remained solidly together, supporting each other as loving companions. They enjoyed their life together, yet it seemed impossible that they could face such hardships with such happiness. How could this possibly be?

It seemed that the answer lay in the fact that they came from similar local families whose own parents had not expected life to be easy. They grew up in a poor rural community where they learned that the key to

what to look forward to within marriage. When you don't get what you expected, small problems assume large proportions, resentments are built up, and the fabric of the relationship erodes.

These people are typical of the confused couples who seek help. But the prospects are not always gloomy. A "truth" about long-term relationships is that it is not the difficulties in our lives that make us unhappy, but how we face those difficulties.

A SUCCESSFUL FORMULA

We've all met couples whose lives seem full of appalling events, who yet appear to be supremely happy. Take Edward and Mara, for example, a couple who married young, had to live with their in-laws while starting their own family, and coped with painful battles against illness. Mara had breast cancer. One child was badly hurt in a serious auto accident, a daughter developed

survival was to pull together, and as children they had seen their own parents overcome differences in order to do this.

By using the methods they had learned from their parents (of problem solving, coping with a partner's anger, and not taking that anger personally) they got through their own dilemmas. Over time they discovered, due to the sheer fact of having survived, that they had acquired a long-term view. Even if more difficulties arose (which they did), they knew they'd get through them.

Let's break down these ingredients. The couple's expectations were realistic. Life wasn't always going to be happy. They expected to have to work for happiness. It wouldn't just materialize.

The couple's communication worked. Each understood what the other was saying, doing, demonstrating. That may sound odd, but since we all come from differing families we all have differing understandings of the same situation. Those of Edward and Mara matched up. Finally, each of them possessed enough self-confidence not to feel under personal attack when the other had a problem or complained about something. And each learned to have faith in the relationship lasting in spite of the difficulties.

THE ADVENTURE OF TACKLING PERSONAL DIFFICULTIES

I would even go further than that. It seems to me that it is the adventure of tackling personal difficulties and doing so successfully that actually nourishes a relationship, keeping it alive. How many long-term couples do you know who are still together but somehow feel dead?

Lucky old Edward and Mara, you may say. They appear to have been born with all the right attributes. What about us ordinary mortals who just don't have these natural advantages? What hope is there for us?

NEW APPROACHES

There's no reason for you to stick to a familiar, established pattern of lovemaking. Occasionally, trying something new can make a thrilling change.

WORKING IT OUT

Happily, the answer is that there is plenty of hope. Even if we haven't had the fortune to be born knowing what works, we can learn it.

In addition, we can always develop self-confidence (if we lack it) and tricks and techniques to help us successfully negotiate the tougher realms of anger and depression. These techniques also help us influence friends and relations positively and encourage the development of personal charisma.

The earlier in a relationship that the partners develop an understanding for each other, the less chance there will be for resentments to fester and love to leave. Ideally, we should try to tune in to such a crash course in personal relations when we first consider commitment. But if we are already struggling with such a commitment, then we could, at the very least, try out some of the enhancement methods described in this book.

The aim of this book, therefore, is to try to help you and your partner identify exactly what you expect from a committed relationship; to explain how to negotiate solutions to any difficulties that may arise; and to show how to turn what is a good relationship into something that is completely exceptional, exciting, and unique.

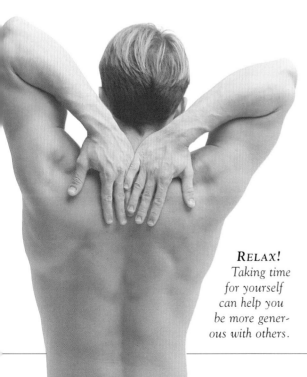

RELAX!
Taking time for yourself can help you be more generous with others.

ABOUT THIS BOOK

In writing this book, my intention has been to provide an insight into the complex emotional side of loving relationships, and in it I show you how to use this insight as a basis for understanding and resolving any difficulties that may arise in your own relationship. No matter what the problem, and how awful it seems, the joy at working it out together, or the relief at being freed from an unhappy situation, easily outweighs the original distress.

One of the best ways to learn how to deal with relationship problems is to take a look at how others have handled similar situations. In this book, therefore, I've made extensive use of the real-life case histories of couples who have come to me for counseling. Every chapter discusses typical problems faced, and each is followed by a detailed description of a case history and how the problem was resolved.

Furthermore, at the end of each chapter is a summary of the relationship-healing exercises and techniques that were used by the couples in the case histories. These are set out as an easy-to-follow guide for you to use in your relationship.

KNOW YOURSELF

Because self-knowledge is a prerequisite for understanding one's relationship with others, the first chapter of the book, "Know Yourself," explains how the seeds of our adult attitudes, morals, views of the world, and personal imperatives are planted within us early in life.

When you know yourself, your strengths and limitations, it becomes far easier to face a problem with calm understanding and a rational, positive approach. This chapter therefore offers simple yet effective methods for discovering how your personal history molded your current personality and ideas about relationships.

Charts and diagrams provide
useful information that
complements the main text

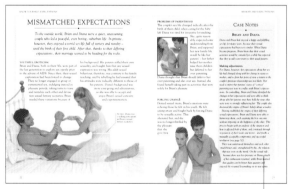

Case Notes boxes give
you further information
and advice

It shows how everyone can gain an insight into his or her belief systems, personal morality, and expectations about how a relationship should work, and how all these are influenced by family background.

KNOW YOUR PARTNER

The second chapter, "Know Your Partner," builds on the information given in the first, and describes how the partners in a relationship can learn to interpret each other's attitudes and emotions, thus developing deeper mutual understanding. It also discusses problems that arise from widely differing backgrounds or conflicting belief systems, and gives useful guidance on how to compromise and make adjustments to minimize any difficulties that may arise.

The exercises suggested for dealing with these problems can be applied, like all the others, to many relationship dilemmas and can help whether a problem is major or minor. The more you know about your partner, the more likely you will be to understand what he or she needs, and to be able to give this to him or her in the most appropriate ways. Even the most stable and loving relationship can be improved. You do not have to wait for a problem to manifest itself before taking steps to minimize its effects.

LEARN TO COMMUNICATE

The key to harmonious personal relationships is good communication. It eliminates misunderstandings, ensures that each partner is aware of the other's likes, dislikes, and wishes, and helps to prevent personal differences escalating into problems and possibly conflict. It also helps partners to build and maintain mutual feelings of warmth and intimacy.

In "Learn to Communicate," I describe the skills we require to be able to talk freely but tactfully to our partners, and I discuss how to be a good listener, for times when your partner needs to talk to you. I then show you how to use these skills to resolve problems by negotiation and compromise, and how to implement any agreed solutions and keep your promises to each other.

Once again, all of the techniques suggested in this chapter can be also used outside the realm of relationship problems, but when they are applied to problems of intimacy the results can be both dramatic and wonderful. The closeness you feel for someone with whom you communicate well can go a long way toward smoothing any disharmony that may arise between you. Unfortunately, poor communication between a couple can lead to damaging misunderstandings.

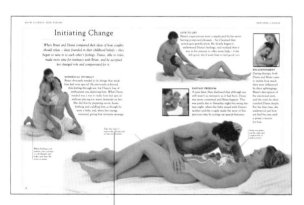

Annotations highlight important features of each case history

Step-by-step methods help you to take practical action

PRACTICAL HELP

Case studies describe a typical problem and show how it can be resolved. In each study, you can follow the troubles of the couple concerned, and learn how therapy exercises helped overcome them. In the Action Plans, the exercises are described in simple steps to help you apply them to your own relationship.

BODY LANGUAGE

One vital but neglected area of communication is the vast amount of nonverbal information we pass to each other, without realizing it.

It has been estimated that in most face-to-face conversations, as much as 65 percent of the information exchanged is communicated nonverbally —that is, by gesture and touch. So knowing what visual and tactile cues to look for when talking to someone can help you get a clearer understanding of his or her feelings.

In the chapter "Body Language," I tell you how to distinguish between welcoming and unwelcoming body language, both in the bedroom and out of it. Through this I hope to help you avoid the upset that can come from misreading signs that are given to you by your partner and show you how to "speak" to your partner with your body. I also

GROWING CLOSE
Although it takes hard work, a strong and loving relationship shines through in every aspect of life.

suggest some simple ways in which you can use touch to convey your feelings of warmth and love to your partner.

ENHANCING INTIMACY

Sexual intimacy has been described as "that wonderful feeling of warmth and caring and tenderness that evolves through lovemaking." Intimacy is certainly what most people look for when entering a relationship, though they may not realize it at the time, and the loss of intimacy is a loss grieved for in a major way by those who have known it at its most intense.

There are, of course, many sides to intimacy that are not associated with sexuality, all of them poignant and touching, but it is often the loss of sexual intimacy that triggers the erosion of a relationship. In "Enhancing Intimacy," I discuss why most of us need sexual intimacy to make our closest relationships work, the social and sexual factors that influence it, and how it can be rediscovered when it has been lost.

STRONG EMOTIONS

Anger, depression, jealousy, and grief are very powerful emotions that can wreak havoc on even the strongest of relationships. The final chapter of the book, "Strong Emotions," suggests practical ways of coping with the intense, and often destructive, forces that can be unleashed by these emotions. Because these emotions are so complex, and often overwhelming, there are extended sections in this chapter on dealing with them.

In this chapter you will find practical advice on approaching and recovering from, or minimizing the effects of, extremes of emotion, whether the sufferer is yourself or your partner. This will not only help you face these problems if they arise; it will allow you to better understand the emotional upheaval that they involve.

KNOW
YOURSELF

Have you ever wondered what makes you react in certain ways to a given situation? Only by discovering what molded your morality, emotional standards, and behavior patterns can you truly understand yourself.

THE NEED FOR SELF-KNOWLEDGE

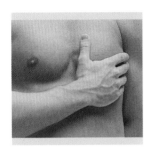

As we grow up, we develop emotionally as well as physically. Our brains expand, taking in all the data that we pick up from our families and later on from our friends. Among the ideas we will take on as gospel will be a view of how marriage works. For most of us, this will be based on the marriage we live with, cheek by jowl, every day of the week—that of our parents.

We tend to expect that our own marriages will follow a pattern similar to our parents' and, unconsciously, this shapes the way we construct our marriages. Because of our expectations (*see page 20*), we expect that all aspects of life will follow patterns like those we knew as children. In a marriage, provided each partner has similar expectations, this works well. Differences, however, can cause problems.

DIFFERING IDEAS

Sometimes partners turn out to have different ideas of what a marriage should consist of, and that is because their expectations have developed diversely in their early years. The man who has seen marriage as an opportunity for wonderful sexual intimacy may find married life hard if his wife views marital sex as simply for having a lot of children. These two expectations about marriage are clearly mismatched.

CONFORMITY

Even when you are aware of these strong influences, and want to break away from them, you may find that circumstances force you to conform. This drift into conformity can present a threat to your relationship, and not just by making you feel frustrated and discontented. It can also lead to you blaming your partner for what you see as your failure to reach your expected ideal. For instance, if you had always wanted to travel widely, and hoped to be able to do so with your partner, you might begin blaming him or her if circumstances—such as work, shortage of money, or family responsibilities—prevented you from doing so.

If only we could know these things in advance we might be able to save ourselves a lot of pain and heartache. That may seem an impossibility, but you can get close to it, and that is where self-knowledge becomes of prime importance. If you can identify your expectations—even if only partially— you can compare them with those of a potential partner. And when you both understand what it is that each of you requires from the other, you will have a clearer insight into your own and each other's needs.

IDENTIFY YOUR EXPECTATIONS

If your ideas about life and how a long-term relationship should function match up with those of your partner, you can give each other the green light. If your ideas do not match up, you have two options. The first is to say farewell, albeit reluctantly. The second is to make allowances for each other—something you can only do successfully when you fully understand your own emotional backdrop and that of your partner.

If each of you can identify what the other is looking for, and you then set out to at least partly satisfy each other's hopes, you may create such good will between you that you find each other's hopes, desires, and goals less pressuring. In addition, having a clear idea of what to do to make each other happy can provide an extra incentive to do so.

CONTRIBUTING FACTORS

There are several distinct factors that contribute to each individual's unconscious views of what constitutes "self," but some of the most important are those that originate in the family background. For example, birth order (see page 26) is important because it affects your interaction with your closest family members, who play a vital part in shaping your ideas and beliefs.

In the same way, the particular code of morality your family subscribes to—which actions, thoughts, and attitudes are right and which are wrong— will be reflected in your own beliefs, even if you rebelled against your family.

INTIMACY THROUGH SELF-KNOWLEDGE
Clear self-knowledge can help strengthen a relationship, allowing you to voice your needs, wants, and expectations easily to your partner.

17

WHAT'S RIGHT FOR ME?

We tend to assume that all our friends possess the same set of morals as ourselves, and even if we go against our basic principles, we believe that we are all going to go against the same ones. Not so. Each individual's morals are unique to that person and are acquired as a result of family beliefs (see page 20) and of the opinions and attitudes of our immediate outside world.

Parents

Friends

Partner(s)

PERSONAL
MORALITY

Education

Work

Beliefs

Religion

MORAL INFLUENCES
Throughout life, our personal moralities are shaped not only by our own thoughts and feelings but also by numerous outside influences.

The morals of an individual, or of a group of people, can seem unusual, but that does not stop them being sincerely held and scrupulously observed, even in the face of ridicule or perhaps condemnation from other people. For instance, there are people who were brought up to believe that it is bad to hurt others by being competitive, and they were taught to return any prizes they won at school. There are people who believe it is wrong to lose your virginity before marriage. There are men and women who would never even think of walking around their own homes naked—not even when completely alone—because their sense of modesty forbids it. And some people have such a highly developed sense of modesty that they are even unwilling to let their partners see them naked.

CHANGING MORALITY

The above examples are to show that we all possess very different sets of morals and that we make a great mistake if we assume others share them. However, if we come from similar backgrounds it is a fair assumption that we will possess similar morals. And indeed, any set of morals is fine, provided it doesn't conflict violently with those of society and of someone you are close to. But morality is not cut and dried. Thirty or forty years ago, many people considered sex before marriage to be immoral. Yet, since then, that belief has changed radically in the Western world. So morals are movable—which means, sadly, that some of us can get very hurt.

CONFLICTING MORALITIES

The issue of what is right and what is wrong gets even more complicated when we look at the question of "good" people. Some "good" people are trying to satisfy their own standards of perfection, and while truly good people sincerely act for the benefit of others, the "do-gooders" may just be satisfying a personal sense of superiority *(see page 37)* that requires them to be "better" than anyone else. Not surprisingly, few of the latter manage to measure up to what may be impossibly high standards, and many become either seriously depressed or depress those around them. Thus, taking the time and making the effort to ferret out each other's personal morality can, at the very least, prevent us from oppressing our nearest and dearest.

AVOIDING CONFLICT

When your partner does something that outrages you, it's hard not to take it personally. It makes sense, therefore, to try to understand where else your partner's behavior might stem from so that you don't take it quite so personally. One of the areas where there are important differences that are not necessarily personal is that of morality. Here is a way of exploring your morality code and that of your partner so that you can decide whether or not you might end up in conflict. This way, you get the chance of understanding how his or her personal morals and beliefs differ from yours (if at all), and give yourself the option either to tolerate the differences or to reconcile them, and so minimize the possibility of conflict.

FACING MORALITY
Polly faced a moral struggle when her husband made her feel that adultery was her only recourse (see pages 144–147).

PERSONAL MORALS

There are certain questions that you can apply to any issue you may be facing, or that you have already come up against. As an example, let's think about attitudes about infidelity. Write down brief answers to these questions. Then compare them with your partner's, and discuss what either or both of you could do to reconcile any differences.

1 What do my morals say about infidelity? (For example, do I believe that there are circumstances where it's all right to sleep with someone other than my partner? Are there circumstances where it's definitely not all right to sleep with someone else? Is it ever all right to sleep with someone else?)

2 Where did my beliefs about infidelity come from? (Parents' opinions, parents' broken marriage, friends' experiences?)

3 How has my religion affected my moral beliefs?

4 How have my ethnicity and culture affected my beliefs?

5 Are my beliefs reasonable?

6 Are my partner's views the same as mine or do they differ?

7 If they do differ, where and how widely?

8 Is there any way of tolerating or reconciling these differences?

9 Could either of us change our behavior to ease the other's hurt?

Identifying which beliefs are reasonable is best done with a partner, because he or she can probably pinpoint contradictions more easily than you, the one who is immersed in set ideas. Try applying similar questions to other moral issues, and remember, it is mature to change your mind if you have seen an old problem with new eyes.

EXPECTATIONS

When we are growing up, we tend to expect that adult life will follow certain patterns, which are based on what we experienced as children. Later, when we form relationships, we often expect that they will be similar to the relationships our parents had. If both partners in a relationship have similar expectations, this works wonderfully. But sometimes each has different ideas.

As children, most of us grow up within a family. The family supplies us with views of ourselves, our roles, a sense of goodness (or badness), and a wider view of the world. Usually, it is certain key figures within the family who influence us most, especially those who are closest to us during the first five years or so of our lives. These are among the most formative years, and much of a person's basic approach to life is learned during that time.

What you see, hear, and take in during those first five years of your life will often have repercussions decades later when you develop relationships of your own and form your own family.

CHANGING BELIEFS

Widely differing circumstances during those early years will produce widely differing adults. A child who was brought up in a children's home, for example, will probably have different personal values than those of a child who was raised in a nuclear family (mother, father, and children). And a child who has been brought up in a large extended family (including grandparents, aunts, uncles, and other relatives) might have much in common with a child brought up in a commune, where several families live together. During those first years we can develop or alter some of the beliefs we've gained, but psychologists think that a child's belief system is formed within the first six or seven years of life. After that, beliefs can change, or be made to change, but often only with difficulty.

Happy, successful marriages are often examples of how beliefs can change. They can give men and women confidence in themselves that they didn't previously possess, and this new confidence represents a change in their beliefs about themselves. Learning to be assertive fosters self-value, which is another change of belief. And often, when the encouragement we

---

Examine the options available to you

Work out what is desirable

Make sure your expectations are realistic

Negotiate with your partner and agree to compromise if necessary

Implement the agreed-upon changes

UNDERSTANDING YOUR EXPECTATIONS
Look at your lifestyle and work out what you really want from it. See where your expectations differ from your partner's, then negotiate those areas to reach a compromise. Once you have agreed, implement the changes in your relationship.

Our most basic attitudes and beliefs are shaped during the early years of our lives, but it is possible to change them.

gain from counseling results in better self-knowledge, we change our personal beliefs again. Despite our ability to change our personal belief systems, differences in expectations about behavior and what life should offer may cause misunderstanding between two people who otherwise love each other dearly. Such a mismatch can easily arise from a need to fulfill unspoken desires or from a reversion to patterns of behavior learned during childhood. And as Brian and Diana found (*see page 22*), the effects of mismatched expectations can be powerful and distressing.

SECRET DESIRES

A relationship can be put under strain when one partner has strong desires or preferences that, for some reason, he or she is unable or unwilling to disclose. Such desires may well be sexual, and a sexual mismatch may arise if lovemaking becomes routine. For example, the man may have settled into a pattern of lovemaking that he believes is as satisfactory for his partner as it is for him, but in fact she longs for something different, such as indulging in dominant/submissive role-playing, mild bondage, or the acting out of sexual fantasies.

NONSEXUAL MISMATCHES

A nonsexual mismatch might be about almost anything, from musical preferences to attitudes to money. For example, one partner might be quite happy living in near-permanent debt, while his or her partner is paranoid about owing a cent. Whether the mismatches are sexual or nonsexual, what matters is that one partner is unaware of the other's needs and so does nothing to accommodate or facilitate them.

PATTERNS OF BEHAVIOR

Even when you think you are getting more or less what you want from your relationship, changing circumstances, such as having a baby, may alter your expectations. These new circumstances may lead either you or your partner (or both of you) to revert to patterns of behavior that you learned in childhood but subsequently forgot about or chose to ignore, and which may have been based on distorted or false beliefs.

We all have options—that is, the choices we are allowed to make and the choices that we allow ourselves to make—whether in our sexual or our social lives. To explore your options and thus improve your sex life (and with it your relationship as a whole) you will need the willing agreement of your partner. You have to be able to state your wishes clearly—but tactfully (*see page 60*)—and then negotiate any necessary compromises with your partner (*see page 72*).

EXPECTATIONS AND CHANGE
When the main thrust of a relationship changes, the couple involved may be disconcerted by the effects this has, especially if both have strong and clearly defined expectations about relationships. Just such a situation nearly brought disaster for Brian and Diana (see pages 22–25).

MISMATCHED EXPECTATIONS

To the outside world, Brian and Diana were a quiet, unassuming couple who led a peaceful, even boring, suburban life. In private, however, they enjoyed a torrid sex life full of variety and novelty— until the birth of their first child. After that, thanks to their differing expectations, their marriage seemed to be heading for the rocks.

YOUTHFUL EROTICISM

Brian and Diana, both in their 30s, were part of the last generation to explore sex openly prior to the advent of AIDS. Since then, their sexual exploration had been forced to change. They no longer engaged in group or extramarital sex, indulging instead in pleasure periods, taking turns to tease and tantalize each other and devise new sexual fantasy scenarios. Brian needed these variations because of his background. His parents stifled their own sexuality, and taught him that any sexual expression was wrong. His adult sexual behavior, therefore, was contrary to his family teaching, and by rebelling he had ensured that his attitudes were radically different from those of his parents. Diana's background was more easy-going and adventurous, so she was able to accept and enjoy Brian's sexual curiosity and experimentation.

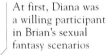

At first, Diana was a willing participant in Brian's sexual fantasy scenarios

PROBLEMS OF PARENTHOOD

The couple's sex life changed radically after the birth of their child, when caring for the baby left Diana too tired for inventive lovemaking.

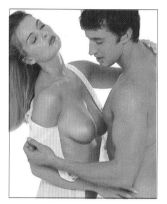

She, quite reasonably, expected some understanding from Brian, and supposed her new family life would be like her parents'—her father helped her mother raise their children but deferred to her over parenting.

Diana thought that Brian should defer to her over parenting and also over sex. Instead, she found herself taking part in activities that were solely for Brian's pleasure.

FORCING CHANGE

Denied sexual treats, Brian's emotions were echoing those he felt in his youth. He felt unimportant and fought back by forcing Diana to be sexually active. This alienated her, and she was no longer thrilled by the pleasure that she gave him.

CASE NOTES

BRIAN AND DIANA

Diana and Brian had enjoyed a happy and fulfilling sex life for many years, because their sexual expectations had been very similar. When Diana became pregnant, Brian knew that their sexual activities would be curtailed for a while but expected that they would soon return to their usual pattern.

Making adjustments

For Diana, however, her expectations about her sex life had changed along with her change in status to mother, and so from her point of view a return to the couple's previous relationship was not likely. Her need to mirror her parents' views of "correct" parenting was now in conflict with Brian's expectations. In counseling, Brian and Diana identified the changes in her expectations and were able to think about why her parents may have held the views that were now so strongly influencing her. The couple also discussed the origins of Brian's beliefs about sexuality.

Having established the origins of their differing sexual expectations, Brian and Diana were able to harmonize them, each attaining the best outcome without imposing on the happiness of the other. This process began with an analysis of the situation and how it affected both of them, and continued through negotiation of their needs and desires, and finally a mutually acceptable compromise and successful resolution (see page 32).

They now understood themselves and each other much better and, strengthened by this, the relationship was soon on the mend. On the sexual side, because there was less pressure on Diana, much of her enthusiasm returned, while Brian learned that quality can be better than quantity and enjoyed the resumed lovemaking on its new terms.

Initiating Change

—•—

When Brian and Diana compared their ideas of how couples should relate—ideas founded in their childhood beliefs—they began to tune in to each other's feelings. Diana, able to relax, made more time for intimacy with Brian, and he accepted her changed role and compensated for it.

NONSEXUAL INTIMACY

Brian obviously needed to do things that made him feel very special. He previously achieved this feeling through sex, but Diana's loss of enthusiasm was depriving him. What Diana needed was a way to make him feel special without placing too many demands on her. She did this by preparing exotic feasts, bathing and cuddling him as though he were a baby, and, when her energy returned, giving him intimate massage.

Take the time to enjoy role playing and acting out fantasies

When bathing your partner, use a sponge or washcloth and make sure that the water is warm

GIVE TO GET

Brian's expectations were complicated by his never having postponed pleasure—he'd learned that action gets gratification. He slowly began to understand Diana's feelings, and realized that it was in his interest to offer more help—if she felt good, she'd want him to feel good, too.

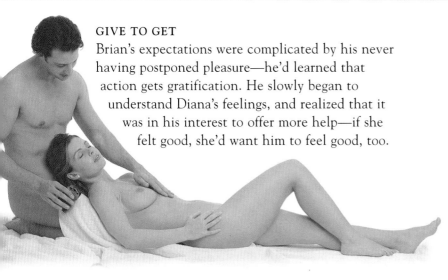

ENLIGHTENMENT

During therapy, both Diana and Brian came to realize how much they were influenced by their upbringings. Brian's description of his emotional pain, and the tears he shed, touched Diana deeply. For the first time, she understood just how sex had become such a prime concern for him.

FANTASY FREEDOM

A year later, they disclosed that although sex still wasn't as extensive as it had been, Diana was more contented and Brian happier. This was partly due to Saturday night becoming fantasy night, when the baby stayed with Diana's mother and the couple made the most of this precious time by acting out special fantasies.

Some sex games can be calm and comfortable as well as erotic

FAMILY INFLUENCES

TWINS
relationships between twins may mirror those of first and younger children

PARENTS

FIRSTBORN
often a high achiever. May be bossy and prone to jealousy

ONLY CHILD
may get used to being the focus of attention

SECOND CHILD
may appear self-contained, is actually very sensitive

THIRD CHILD
independent, can be aggressive and emotionally needy

FAMILY, CHARACTER, AND BIRTH ORDER
The order in which you and your siblings were born directly influences your relationship with other family members and your personality.

Sibling rivalry is a well-known phenomenon, but brothers and sisters have other influences on one another.

One of the keys to how couples interact may be how each interacted with his or her parents and siblings (if any). For example, a bossy elder sister may well form a relationship with someone who was a pushy younger brother—who had a bossy elder sister of his own.

The relationship a child has with his or her family is greatly influenced by birth order—whether the child is, say, the eldest, youngest, or middle child. Birth order also affects the way a person views the world, both as a child and as an adult, and how he or she relates to the influential adults in early life. To discover who had the greatest influence on your young life, draw out your own family constellation (*see page 32*). Many people find the conclusions they draw from a family constellation relate to birth order.

BIRTH ORDER AND RELATIONSHIPS

One of the things that often happens in a marriage or other loving relationship is that once each partner has adapted to the novelty of the other and settled down, both may unconsciously reenact old patterns of behavior. One theory is that this helps improve our feelings about ourselves through reexperiencing certain childhood relationships. A terrible childhood relationship with a brother, for example, may cause old feelings of jealousy and anger to be passed on to a partner later in life.

FIRSTBORN AND PARENTAL GUIDANCE

A firstborn or eldest child, like an only child (*see opposite*), may bear the brunt of parental mistakes and inexperience, and may get used to being the sole focus of attention, reacting with distress if that attention stops. A firstborn child will often be a high achiever, striving, perhaps tense, bossy, and competitive, and possibly prone to jealousy and insecurity.

He or she will probably also have been given undivided parental attention and so may find the birth of the next child unsettling and disillusioning, because much of the love and attention once taken for granted is redirected at the new baby. Insecurity and jealousy can easily creep into such a situation. Parents who don't know any better may expect too much, too fast, from their first child and may encourage him or her to take part in activities that are overly complex or mature. This may lead to pockets of precociousness in the child that disguise "raw" areas of its developing character, areas in which it is extremely anxious because of being made to learn and live at a pace that feels out of control.

SECOND CHILD AND ESTABLISHED PARENTING
In most cases, a second child has to put up with ideas of parenting shaped by the needs of an elder sibling, whose character may be very different from his or her own. This can cause difficulties in the psychological fit between the child and the parents, and in self-defense the child may cope by distancing him- or herself emotionally. In this case, the child may give the impression of being very self-contained, but in reality he or she may be extremely sensitive. The key to understanding the needs and emotions of the second child is to realize that he or she may feel inferior to the first, and will need particular attention, sympathy, and reassurance if this feeling is to be remedied. Despite this, a second child will often prove to be a supremely sensual adult.

THIRD CHILD—THE BABY OF THE FAMILY
Although independent, a third child may often be more aggressive and emotionally needy than older siblings. As the youngest, though, especially if physically appealing, he or she may be babied by the whole family (unless, of course, a fourth child arrives). This multiple attention can give the third child a sense of special importance, but it may also mean that much in a relationship is taken for granted. Since the opinions and feelings of a third child may often be overlooked, the child could doubt the validity of its own experiences.

This may lead a third child to become uncertain about his or her judgment and to compensate for this, when an adult, by setting up very structured routines to maintain a sense of self-worth. If these routines are suddenly removed, the adult may feel terribly adrift.

TWINS
Although each of a pair of twins will gain support from the presence of the other, the younger may resent the priorities that an elder child often receives, through accident of birth. If the older twin is a girl, she may baby the younger (whether that twin is a boy or a girl), which can create a subservient, overly dependent person who simultaneously resents this dependence. On the other hand, the younger may feel no need to assume responsibility for anything because the elder always takes it.

ONLY CHILD
An only child is one who has been brought up in a household where there are no other children. Being always in the limelight may make an only child self-assured, but it also has its down side.

An only child gets used to being the focus of attention and may become self-absorbed and seem dismissive of others. And an only child, having no siblings to interact with and to learn from, might also become unduly close to—and influenced by—one or both parents.

ACQUIRED INHIBITIONS
Julia, an only child, had too close a relationship with her mother, who was inhibited by phobias. She acquired some of her mother's inhibitions, which impaired her relationship with her husband (see pages 28–31).

INHIBITIONS

Julia, an only child, had opted to remain a virgin until marriage. Her husband, Paul, had put that down to shyness. But her embarrassment about showing her body and acting in any openly sexual manner was putting a strain on their relationship.

SHYNESS AND EMBARRASSMENT

Julia was very shy and embarrassed about lovemaking, but her sexual responses were otherwise quite normal. "Once she gets going, she's fine," Paul said, "But it's starting that's so difficult. And although she really loves oral sex, she is usually horrified if I suggest it."

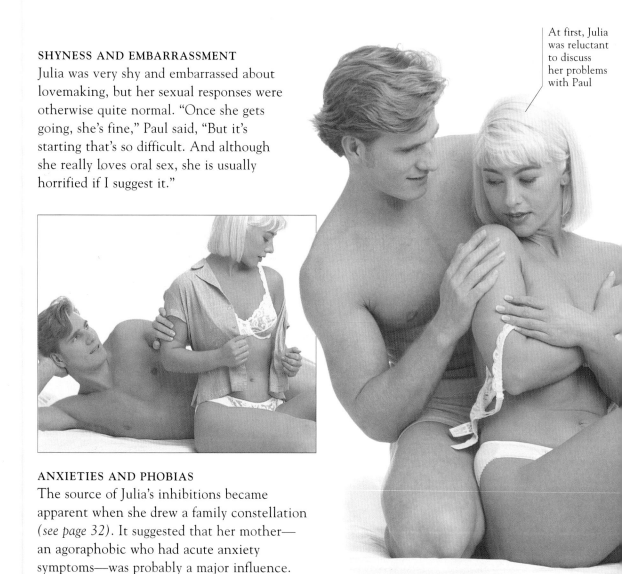

At first, Julia was reluctant to discuss her problems with Paul

ANXIETIES AND PHOBIAS

The source of Julia's inhibitions became apparent when she drew a family constellation (*see page 32*). It suggested that her mother—an agoraphobic who had acute anxiety symptoms—was probably a major influence.

INHIBITED RESPONSES

"I do love Paul," Julia said. "And actually I do like sex with him. I just don't seem to be able to show it. I don't know why I'm so tense, but I know that sex was a source of problems for my parents." These problems seemed linked to her mother's phobias, and in fact Julia was herself agoraphobic, but less so than her mother.

Paul had been sympathetic toward his wife, and attributed this to his family background. His childhood had been happy and relaxed, in a home where the family attitude had been to "enjoy what you've got." It was that same attitude that allowed him to appreciate his wife, inhibitions and all.

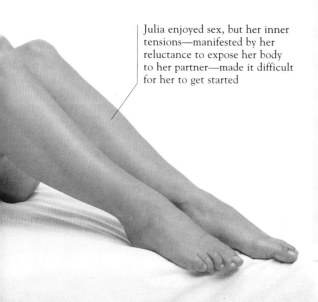

Julia enjoyed sex, but her inner tensions—manifested by her reluctance to expose her body to her partner—made it difficult for her to get started

CASE NOTES

JULIA AND PAUL

For Julia, the pleasures of sex were marred by the tension and embarrassment that preceded it. Her inhibited approach to sex contrasted sharply with the relaxed, easy-going sexuality of her husband, Paul, and turned out to be part of a more general set of anxieties and phobias that she shared, in part, with her mother. It was also, perhaps, the reason she had chosen to remain a virgin until she married.

As sometimes happens with an only child, Julia had been unduly influenced by her mother. When Julia talked about her, it became apparent that her mother was a stranger to spontaneity and overt affection.

Major influences
The first real clue to the origin of Julia's problems came when she drew her family constellation (see page 32), a counseling tool that provides useful insights into a person's childhood relationship with key members of his or her family. Without siblings to share the attention, Julia's constellation showed her mother to be the major influence on her early life, and further counseling revealed the extent of her mother's phobias.

Guilt-free pleasure
Julia consulted a psychiatrist for help with her anxieties, and once she had made sufficient progress with overcoming them she was able to begin dealing with her sexual inhibitions. In addition to more counseling, she followed a self-pleasuring routine involving moves such as caressing her body, plus masturbation and indulging in sexual fantasies. This taught her about her body's physical responses, helped her learn to relax and enjoy them without feeling guilty, and boosted her sexual self-confidence.

Overcoming Inhibitions

Using the family constellation exercise (see page 32),
Julia had been able to see how she had learned her inhibitions
from her mother. This insight meant that she and Paul were then
able to progress with overcoming this anxiety about sex with
patience and greater understanding.

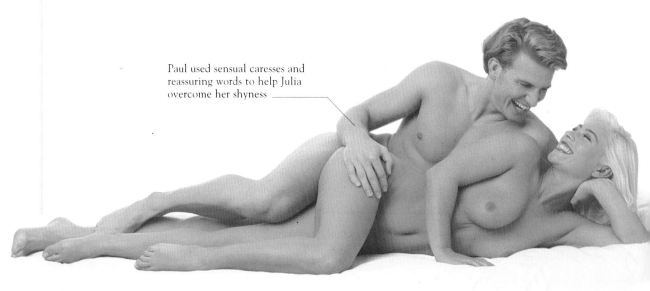

Paul used sensual caresses and
reassuring words to help Julia
overcome her shyness

SPONTANEOUS ENJOYMENT

Julia had come from the kind of tight-knit family
where the drive for respectability can get in the way
of spontaneous enjoyment and warmth; she was also
suffering from inhibitions learned from her mother.
Fortunately, Paul's parents had been so comfortable
with each other that displays of affection were
more common than those of temper, so there
was enough warmth in his background to melt
through much of the problem.

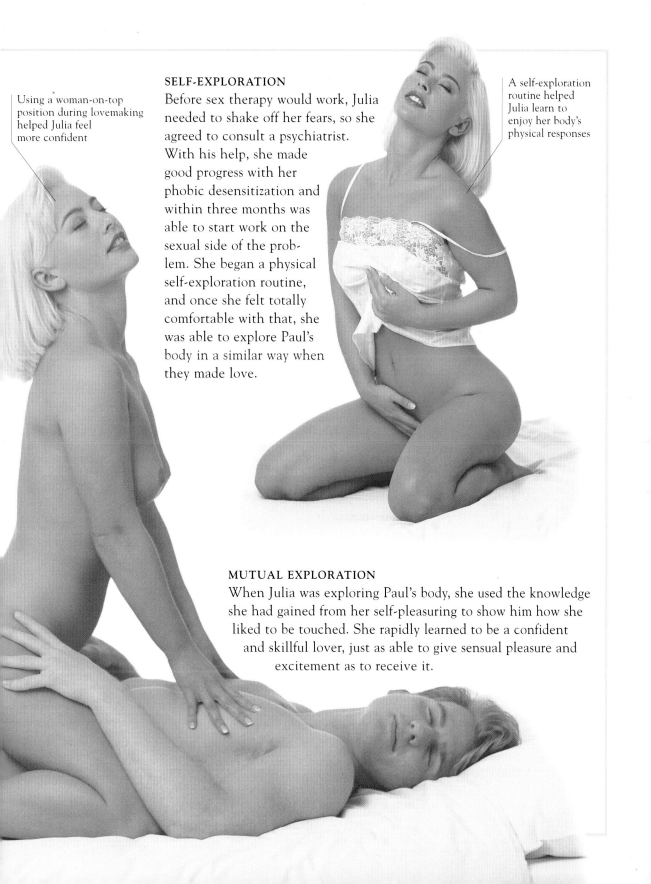

Using a woman-on-top position during lovemaking helped Julia feel more confident

SELF-EXPLORATION

Before sex therapy would work, Julia needed to shake off her fears, so she agreed to consult a psychiatrist. With his help, she made good progress with her phobic desensitization and within three months was able to start work on the sexual side of the problem. She began a physical self-exploration routine, and once she felt totally comfortable with that, she was able to explore Paul's body in a similar way when they made love.

A self-exploration routine helped Julia learn to enjoy her body's physical responses

MUTUAL EXPLORATION

When Julia was exploring Paul's body, she used the knowledge she had gained from her self-pleasuring to show him how she liked to be touched. She rapidly learned to be a confident and skillful lover, just as able to give sensual pleasure and excitement as to receive it.

ACTION PLAN

HARMONIZING YOUR NEEDS as a couple is a two-step process. First, identify your expectations about life and relationships by looking at what has influenced you to have certain views on life situations. Second, trace the source of these expectations with family constellations and character profiles. Gaining this self-knowledge is only the beginning, and your partner must do the same before you can progress.

UNDERSTANDING EXPECTATIONS

When your expectations do not coincide with your partner's, the first thing to do is clarify your beliefs and expectations. Look at those areas where you and your partner disagree and work out why by studying the following points:

- *Ask your partner to identify any distortions that he or she sees in your expectations.*
- *Think back to your early beliefs—did any distortions have clear origins?*
- *Ask yourself if your relatives may have held the views that influenced you in these areas and ask, "Are these views relevant to me today?"*

If you feel comfortable with your personal expectations, you can begin to negotiate.

- *Make sure your expectations are realistic and reasonable.*
- *Tactfully make your wishes clear.*
- *Listen to your partner's views.*
- *Be willing to compromise and make changes, too.*

Harmonizing your expectations is not necessarily a one-time exercise. If your personal circumstances (or those of your partner) change, your expectations may also change. If that happens, repeat the exercises together.

DRAWING FAMILY CONSTELLATIONS

It is important also to understand the impact your family had on you as a child. Imagine that you are a star and that your relations are neighboring stars.

- *Picture your relations. Place those with the most influence on you very close to your star, and those with less, farther away.*
- *See which areas of each individual affected your beliefs and attitudes.*
- *Don't forget to include other people who were important to you—your best friends, for example.*
- *When you've finished, ask your partner to draw his or her family constellation.*
- *Compare your charts.*

- *Talk through the relationships you've drawn, starting with those of most importance and working your way to the least important.*
- *Note the character traits of those closest to you, and ask yourselves how these people influenced you.*
- *Pay attention to the distances you have placed each character in your constellations. This has meaning. For instance, if your mother ends up on the outer rim of your constellation, does that mean that you discount her, or that she discounted you?*

Now you can progress and go on to assemble character profiles for yourself and your partner.

- *Using a scale of, say, 0 to 20, assess your partner's levels of self-confidence, ability to take action, stress levels, self-control, levels of frustration, and ability to relate to members of the opposite sex. Give him or her a score for each.*
- *Compare each other's scores, especially the highest and lowest, and judge these against your family constellations to see in which areas your families most influenced you.*

At this stage you can begin to work on any problem areas in your relationship. Start with areas you both feel are least difficult. The experience of problem-solving that this gives you will help you deal with any more difficult areas.

KNOW YOUR PARTNER

*Understanding how your partner views the
world, and finding out where these views have
come from and how flexible your partner is
about them, will help you minimize
misunderstandings in your life together.*

YOUR PARTNER'S EMOTIONS

For all the same reasons that it makes sense to delve into your own upbringing and personal beliefs, so too is it sensible to gain insight into those of your lover. How else can you compare your beliefs if only one of you knows what you are talking about or looking for? Ask your partner, therefore, to read the previous section and work with you jointly on this one.

We tend to make so many assumptions about each other that the truth about a partner often produces surprises. Do you know, for example, how your partner finds meaning from life? Or whether he or she does this in the same way that you do? Have you realized what nurturing skills he or she has? Or considered how his or her expectations about the future differ from yours?

Take the case of a partner who was raised to believe firmly in marriage as an institution, yet rebelled against the tight control of his or her family by choosing a very alternative way of life, refusing ever to marry or to commit to fidelity. It would be easy for this person's partner to assume that such declarations of rebellion were heartfelt and true.

What both parties may indeed fail to appreciate is how much that partner might need a secure home base in the future, or need the strong sense of duty he or she would feel toward a child—even though that person's original lifestyle had not led anyone to expect these needs.

It is possible to see how some partners might be thrown into confusion when a romantic but wild figure such as this is transformed into a pillar of the local community. It illustrates perfectly the desirability of getting to know your partner's background in some detail.

PERSONALITY PRIORITIES

As we grow up, coping with our particular families, we develop our own personal methods for surviving them. Some psychologists believe that we develop certain aspects of our character at the expense of others in order to cope. This gives us a bias toward certain kinds of behavior, which become priorities. Bossy elder children, for example, go for control. The problem is that control can turn into overcontrol (*see pages 62–65*), which can seriously damage later relationships.

Other people seek comfort and will do anything for a quiet life. This can make it extremely difficult to get them to talk about problems because they immediately try to avoid the discussion.

There are others still who seem unable to avoid head-on conflict. The bull-in-the-china-shop approach won't work, yet this doesn't stop some otherwise attractive people from adopting it.

This section, therefore, expands on two more early life situations that feed our childhood personality. These are personality priorities, such as the need for control, and your view of the world outside marriage, which is especially useful to men and women in mixed-culture marriages.

THE VALUE OF SIMILARITY

There is great value in marrying someone of a similar background and upbringing. It means that, statistically, a couple stands a much better chance of surviving together over the years. Research from the United States in the 1970s showed that a marriage of opposites was less likely to succeed than a marriage of like-minded people.

This isn't to say you can't gain a great deal from each other's differences. One of the issues in a long-term partnership is surviving them. They may be both emotional and behavioral—one usually leads to another.

DEALING WITH DIFFERENCES

Approaching such differences positively, weighing the good against the bad, adds stability to a relationship.

Sexually, these matters may show up as different expectations in bed. One Asian client expected his American wife to have a pill that would cure his impotence. She was baffled by this and believed that she was being blamed for something outside her experience. Similarly, George (*see pages 46–49*) had not expected his wife to be so passionate and active in bed because he had thought that a virgin was unlikely to be so sexual.

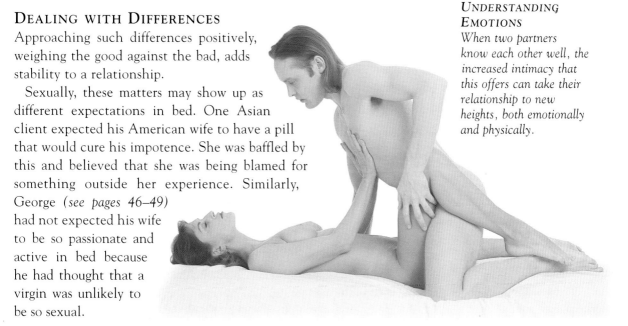

UNDERSTANDING
EMOTIONS
When two partners know each other well, the increased intimacy that this offers can take their relationship to new heights, both emotionally and physically.

BEHAVIOR PATTERNS

PLEASERS
eager to please,
but expect
reward

COMFORT
SEEKERS
look for an easy life,
perhaps because
of a pampered
childhood

SUPERIOR
PEOPLE
always have to
be right, but really
need love and
reassurance

CONTROLLERS
always need to
control situations,
or their emotions,
or other people

PERSONALITY TYPES
*If you recognize any of
these character traits in
yourself, try to ensure
that no single aspect
of any one of them
becomes exclusive in
your personality.*

**CONTROL THROUGH
DECISION MAKING**
Understanding it's all
right to change your
mind, when all your life
you've believed this to
be a sign of weakness,
can be a revelation.
Indeed, changing your
mind and understanding
that it's normal and
human to make mistakes
are often clear signs
of maturity.

*One major psychological theory states that in order to carve out
our place in the world as children we organize ourselves around
our "personality priorities." These may include traits such as
trust, control, or a desire to please and comfort. Discovering
your partner's personality priority can help you understand his or
her deep-seated feelings and how to help if these cause problems.*

Some men and women do their best to please, while others constantly seek
reassurance and comfort; there are those who act as though they are
superior and those who always need to be in control. Although everyone
is different, people whose personality priorities overwhelm all other
aspects of their personalities need understanding and tactful handling.

PLEASERS

Because they can't seem to do enough for you, some men and women are
a delight to be with. Of course, provided they don't expect to be rewarded
for their efforts, there's nothing wrong with this. Unfortunately, however,
many "pleasers" do expect rewards, because they believe that they can earn
or buy love and affection. They are particularly anxious to avoid rejection,
so qualifying for appreciation like this is all-important to them. Sadly, the
exercise is self-defeating, as they can never be sure if they themselves are
loved or if it's just their gifts.

COMFORT SEEKERS

People who can be termed "comfort seekers" tend to want to avoid stress
at all costs. This is often because they have been given a pampered and
spoiled childhood and cannot, as a consequence, discriminate between
real needs and mere wants. As adults, such need for immediate gratification causes them to feel frustration pretty easily.

A comfort seeker will go to great lengths to avoid this stress, often using
methods of avoidance to do so. An extreme but classic comfort seeker may
actually walk out on a relationship and set up with someone new rather than
confront the problems in an attempt to resolve them.

Helping a comfort seeker to change is extremely difficult, because any
pressure makes him or her run, dodge the issue, postpone the talk, or find
something more urgent to do rather than face the issue. It may be helpful to

point out to them that one of the best ways of reducing stress is to act responsibly. It's also wise to concentrate your thoughts on the positive sides of a situation rather than dwelling on the negative ones.

SUPERIORITY

Some men and women seem intent on appearing superior to others. They act this out by mothering or fathering their partners, by always having to be right, or by bragging constantly. One of the best methods of dealing with a person who is behaving in this way is to give him or her reassurance. Make it clear how much he or she is loved and valued. This is effective because the striving for superiority is often closely linked with distressing feelings of inferiority, which are often the cause of a maddening need always to know best.

CONTROL

There are three ways in which a person can be a "control freak." One is to use rigid self-control, never giving in to emotions, which will make that person very cold in relationships. Another way is to control situations. At its most extreme, this can lead to personal breakdown if, for example, the situation is in fact uncontrollable. The third, and most common, way is an attempt to control other people. Others invariably react to this with anger. A classic sexual example of this is the person who always has to make the moves in bed and who dislikes signs of initiative, or indeed signs of any passion that does not accord with his or her own ideas.

RELEASING CONTROL
When Andrew (see pages 102–105) realized that the difficulties he and girlfriend Vicki were having stemmed partly from his feelings of losing autonomy and control in his home and his life, the way was clear for them to work toward a happier relationship and a more secure home life.

LEARNING TO CONTROL REACTIONS

Use this three-point plan to help you deal with a hurtful or difficult situation— for example, feeling taken for granted. First suggested by the great psychologist, Alfred Adler (1870 – 1937), the plan has helped many people over the years.

1 *Remember that you are affected less by the events that happen in your life (which you often cannot control) than by your attitude toward those events (which you have more chance of "choosing"). It is often your reaction to an event that causes you pain, rather than the event itself.*

2 *If you have been reacting with great emotional drama to a situation, stop yourself from doing so and tell yourself that the drama is only making the feelings worse.*

3 *Instead of dwelling on a problem and letting it get you down, think of something more positive and pleasant—plan a better future for yourself.*

These steps are but a small beginning, but they can save you from spiraling down into depression when things go wrong. Thinking positively keeps you from being preoccupied with your problems and puts you back in control of your emotions—and your life.

UNDERSTANDING EMOTION

In recent polls asking men and women what they looked for in a marriage, most of them replied that they sought personal happiness and a sense of "growth." This is in some contrast to older notions of marriage, where nuptial bliss was seen as an alliance of emotions and a working environment in which to run a household and raise children. And it ignores the importance of understanding each other's emotions.

In addition to being breadwinner, companion, and parent, partners are now expected to provide and improve personal feelings for each other. This means that there's one heck of a lot of pressure put on partners to create good times. Of course, it is possible to experience great love and joy with a marvelous partner, but this will depend on your partner's personality as well as your own. If one partner makes the other happy, it must be reciprocated, requiring both partners to have independent, positive lives.

Seeing beneath your partner's surface emotions can help you gain insight into his or her true feelings and beliefs.

The distinguished psychologist Alfred Adler reckoned that our whole lives are built around feeling good enough. He believed that we achieved these "good enough" feelings through three main concerns: those of occupation (how useful we feel in the world); of social relationships (the company we enjoy with friends); and of intimate relationships. His followers advanced this theory by assessing what was actually responsible for making us feel great or terrible. They concluded that self-worth, meaning from life, nurturing, and leisure were platforms for life experience.

COPING WITH UNCERTAINTY

If you aren't too sure of yourself, coping with marriage problems can be tricky. One woman sought therapy after years of marriage and revealed that she had never had an orgasm; she had always been too scared to mention it. Assertiveness training helped her experience orgasm and feel better about her new, stronger self.

NURTURING

It may be that nurturing offers more joy to women than men, which is not to deny that many men get a wonderful buzz from taking care of others. Nurturing is a combination of caring, encouragement, and facilitating. A partner is *not* being nurturing if he or she does everything for the other because independence and self-sufficiency are denied. Sexual nurturing may include the patience to help a partner discover his or her sexual response, managing without sex on nights when a partner can't or won't be sexually active, and endorsing a sexual activity that is particular to your partner, without necessarily having to take part in it yourself. For many people, this evokes warmth, love, and security.

Probably the best way in which a couple can nurture each other is to spend some time parenting each other, as long as this doesn't become overpowering. Most of us want a partner, not a parent or a child.

LEISURE

In a time when personal achievement, financial and career success, and the stresses of job pressure loom over us, looking at leisure constructively may seem redundant in itself. But leisure possesses its own worth because it provides us with extra facilities for personal growth. It also allows us to experience a very different set of emotions—most notably relaxed ones. Friendship, love, and sex rate highly among many leisure activities.

SELF-WORTH

Your own sense of worth can be so closely identified with loving and being loved that it can be hard sometimes to see it any other way. The basis for confidence is having been loved as a child. If a person hasn't had this, it's still possible to gain self-worth from intimate friends and lovers. Self-worth is often an issue for women who find it hard to experience orgasm. In therapy groups, low self-confidence is a common denominator, and this isn't just due to poor sex. On exploring family history, the low self-esteem is invariably a product of verbally abusive parents, or discouraging parents, or parents who offered no support when it was needed.

Good sex isn't the only thing in a person's life that can make him or her happy. Many people who have had fabulous lovemaking experiences are able to equate those feelings with other instances when respect and self-worth have produced a similar glow.

GETTING MEANING FROM LIFE

There are so many ways to get meaning from life that the list is endless. From those early, earnest adolescent debates about good and evil to the joy you feel as you cradle the lover in your arms, anything goes.

Perhaps finding the meaning in life is most important at times when you feel that you have none. On the sexual side, such depression may cause the sufferer to feel uninterested in a much-loved partner, or perhaps the sex act itself feels so dull there no longer seems any point to it. Paying attention to the subdued feelings will probably have the side effect of removing the sexual difficulty (see pages 134–139).

FACING THE TRUTH
For Aline and Robert (see pages 40–43), discovering the truth behind Aline's cruel comments soon led them to an understanding that saved their marriage.

NO GOOD IN BED?

A cruel remark hits below the belt, particularly when it casts aspersions on a person's ability in bed. When Aline, a strong-willed woman five years older than her husband, criticized his sexual performance, Robert reacted with extreme depression.

Aline would excite Robert by initiating sex

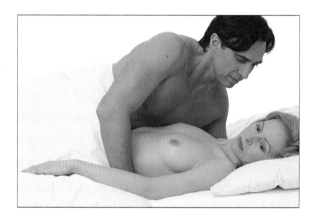

PERFORMANCE ANXIETY
Robert was so depressed he was considering leaving his wife. "She actually courted me and I loved it, but after we had our twins she lost interest in me. She's continually making subtle put-downs, usually when we've just made love. In other words, I don't satisfy her. I think I've always been anxious about it, but now it's too much. I can't go on like this."

CHANGING NEEDS
Aline found Robert extremely arousing early in their relationship. "The great aphrodisiac was that Robert respected my judgment and saw me as a sexy older woman. I found Robert's sexual passivity very exciting, then."

RECOGNIZING VULNERABILITY

Aline didn't appear to be too worried by her husband's declared intention of leaving. Nevertheless, she did admit, "I don't want Robert to leave. But I would like him to stop moping around. I know he sees me as this incredibly powerful woman but, in fact, I'm vulnerable, too. As for the sex, well, he's not the most exciting lover I've ever had. But I've always enjoyed the familiarity of sex with him."

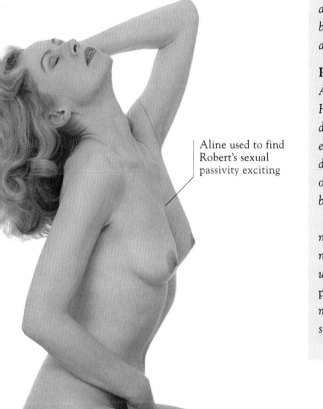

Aline used to find Robert's sexual passivity exciting

CASE NOTES

ALINE AND ROBERT

Aline's part in her relationship with Robert had changed from playing a dominant role—which Robert had found arousing—to a kind of bullying that was making him so depressed he was thinking of leaving her. When they first sought counseling—at Robert's suggestion—Aline seemed relatively unconcerned about the prospect of her marriage breaking up, possibly because she thought that Robert would back down and plead with her to give it another chance.

Personality types

Aline's problem had three interlocking components. Her air of superiority was actually camouflage for a deep-seated feeling of inferiority; this feeling was exacerbated by her belief that her attractiveness had diminished since the birth of her twins; and her sense of inferiority was the legacy of a childhood dominated by her harsh and aggressive father.

To overcome the problem with her marriage, it was necessary for Aline to come to terms with her true nature and its causes, and for each of the partners to understand the other's dominant personality type (see page 56). Then, as they set about rebuilding their marriage, they could concentrate on each other's strengths and make allowances for any vulnerabilities.

Renewing Interest

Through therapy, Aline was able to discover what lay at the root of her behavior and take positive steps to save the marriage. Robert took it upon himself to be more supportive of Aline, although her aggressive behavior had previously made this seem unnecessary. She responded lovingly.

CAMOUFLAGING FEELINGS

Aline revealed that her father had been a very difficult man who ridiculed everyone around him. Thus, Aline spent much of her childhood trying to feel good about herself in the face of this destructive parent. When it was explained that Aline was acting "superior" because she was actually feeling inferior, both partners looked thoughtful. That evening the couple made love for the first time in weeks. Robert felt stronger and Aline more needy.

Reassurance and trust can help both partners feel warm toward each other

UNDERSTANDING SELF-DOUBT

At the next counseling session, Aline was able to reveal that she had been depressed about what she saw as her lack of attractiveness since the birth of the twins. She felt these doubts had triggered old behavior patterns. She didn't actually apologize for her behavior, but Robert told me she was actively seeking sex with him again.

PLEASURE IN PROGRESS

Over the next six months the couple worked hard to improve things. Each was asked to behave in a way that allowed the other to feel wanted and desired. This didn't have to be focused only on sex; it could affect any aspect of behavior. Reminding Aline from time to time about the perils of falling into the trap of "superiority mode" led her to make good progress, albeit with an occasional snag. Robert, however, both looked and felt stronger. And Aline's rediscovered need for sex meant she would initiate it when he least expected it.

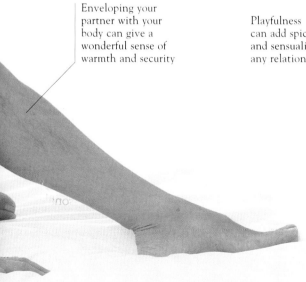

Enveloping your partner with your body can give a wonderful sense of warmth and security

Playfulness can add spice and sensuality to any relationship

DIFFERING ATTITUDES

Each individual's view of the world outside the family depends on the time and place in which they are born. If we were Amazon Indians, for example, our world would be the forest. We would see any place outside the forest as the dream world, not as the real world. This notion illustrates what differing concepts we are capable of holding and that we each have our own unique angle.

A teenager in the West takes for granted computers, sophisticated household appliances, both parents at work, regular changes in environment (parents moving the home when following work), and an expectation that the world will provide entertainment (in the form of movies and television). Such a view of the world modifies our perception of "self." If we see the world as rewarding we may become lazy or bored. If it appears aggressive or dangerous, we may become furtive or withdrawn. If we believe that it offers us unlimited power we may become manic or burdened with responsibility.

Race

Culture

Education

COMMON AREAS OF DIFFERENCE

Social Class

Politics

Nationality

Religion

VIEWS AND BELIEFS
Although there are many areas in life where partners discover they differ, there are also many instances in which these differences are not only surmountable, but highly stimulating.

THE PROBLEMS WITH DIFFERENT BACKGROUNDS

Psychological research shows that a happy and lasting marriage is more likely if our partner has a character and background similar to our own. This doesn't mean there's no hope of achieving it with someone from a different background—often the differences will help maintain interest. It's a good idea, however, to understand those differences so, if necessary, you can make allowances for them.

Comparing differing views makes sense. It helps to realize and negotiate problem areas before problems themselves arise. If you're comfortable and flexible with friends of other races or cultures, you probably find it easier than many others to adapt to different customs. You may find, however, that when your own beliefs are questioned you may react less flexibly than you anticipated. It must be clear that understanding your values and where they come from is not in any way to discard them, but when your values are in conflict with your partner's, then it may be that you should ask yourself if your original interpretations, gathered as a child, were correct.

Many people find it hard to accept that their own highly personal values, which may have been held unchanged for many years, may be outdated and biased. Yet, until these values are examined and either accepted or discarded, any relationship may suffer the problems of blind belief.

REALIZING DIFFERENCES

It can be difficult to accept that other cultures can have equally entrenched beliefs and systems that to one may seem quite natural while to another may appear brutal, unjust, or ridiculous. Unfortunately, blinkered attitudes, or the sudden realization of the impact that beliefs can have, cause the majority of problems in relationships that cross cultural boundaries. Many Western women who marry Eastern men, for example, find it difficult to accept and adopt the strict social and marital rules that their husband's culture demands. Not finding out before the marriage can cause grave problems later on.

Although it is important to understand how your partner's background may affect your relationship, you must also understand the impact it will have on your day-to-day life. The realization that a partner's cultural background may prove to be more important than yours, or than you, can cause terrible pain.

Where you may be polite or caring enough not to have highlighted the failings of your partner's cultural beliefs, he or she may not be so understanding of yours. Sometimes problems can arise over such basic things as eating, working, or equality within the relationship.

ADJUSTING TO EACH OTHER

The most important aspect of settling into a long-term relationship is to believe that your partner is really the person you want. This is particularly important in a mixed-culture relationship as neither partner, no matter how willing to compromise, will become a different person.

If one partner is going too far in making allowances for cultural and ethnic differences, that partner may soon find that he or she has lost sight of commonsense judgment. In George and Polly's relationship (*see pages 46–49*), for example, although Polly was forced to compromise her free expression of sexual enjoyment, her marriage managed to work because counseling taught George that if he wanted to survive living and working in the United States, instead of his native Greece, he must modify his behavior. He did this by starting at home, where he learned that he didn't have to throw tantrums in order to be taken seriously.

In the majority of cases the initial problem can be resolved with a little compromise. It is unlikely that two people will become too deeply involved with each other if they have no positive "gut feeling" between them. Insight into each other's family life helps to foster feelings of sympathy.

If a family is unsupportive of a "mixed" marriage, in this age of technology when so many of us have friends across the world, close friends may take on a very supportive role as two cultures settle down to living together. Above all else, it's understanding in the first place and compromise afterward that makes a marriage between different cultures exciting.

MAKING ADJUSTMENTS
George and Polly (see pages 46–49) realized that their differences in expectations were driving them apart. A little understanding on both sides soon revived their relationship.

CULTURE CLASH

•

We all have unique ways of expressing ourselves in bed.
In Polly's case, she dropped her outwardly demure
manner, becoming an uninhibited lover. George,
attracted by her virginal demeanor, was
suspicious of her behavior.

SUSPICIOUS MINDS

Most men would be thrilled to find ardor lying hidden,
but George viewed Polly's sexuality with deep suspicion.
To cap his doubts, Polly quickly became pregnant despite
taking the contraceptive pill. George quickly concluded
he had been duped: "I think she is passing someone else's
child off on me." Yet, despite
demanding a divorce, he could
not resist making love to her.

PICTURE PERFECT

It was easy to see why George
was attracted to Polly, the
perfect foil for him. She
looked picture perfect,
quietly dressed, pretty,
and soft-voiced. She was
the epitome of good breeding
and modesty. But she was a
woman for whom a classically mild
exterior disguised an extremely
sensual nature. All she had been
waiting for was someone to unlock
her passion, and that someone
was her husband of three
months, George.

The sexual release
Polly found with
her husband belied
her modesty and
refinement

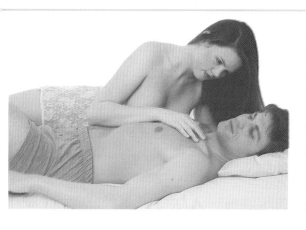

TANTRUMS

George was a volatile young man who raged and threatened when he was angry. Polly, who had every reason to feel like the injured party, was forced to pacify him and generally behave like his mother. "I've done everything I can to reassure him," she said. "But our lovemaking is ruined. Any spontaneity has gone. I now feel that anything I do will cause trouble. Yet George needs comfort so we just keep going."

UNABLE TO STOP

It was Polly who had sought counseling because George had reached a stage of hysteria and was demanding that she get an abortion. Polly did not want to do this, but she found herself in an emotional trap. An abortion would calm her

husband, but at great emotional cost to her. If she didn't, she feared losing him, which was not what she wanted either. The whole issue seemed suspect for the very good reason that George was still making love to his wife every night. What was going on here?

Polly no longer felt free to be dominant and enjoy the pleasures of sex with George, but nevertheless wanted to please him

Facing Reality

When a man criticizes his wife's sexual technique on the one hand, but demands more lovemaking on the other, there is a hidden issue of control. But whose control? George appeared smooth and sophisticated, but underneath he felt vulnerable and insecure.

CHILDHOOD TRAINING

Attitudes that had been established early in their childhoods were causing severe differences between George and Polly. Because he had set ideas about the correct approach to sex that a virgin should

have, George interpreted his wife's innocent behavior as something other. Polly, on the other hand, had learned to suppress most of her emotions including her sexuality—and that was soon released after marriage.

UPBRINGING

George had been brought up in a hysterical household where dramatic scenes got attention, but now his childish tantrums were destroying his marriage. Nevertheless, Polly craved his fiery temperament to make up for her own "cool" upbringing.

MAKING PROGRESS

The couple soon agreed that the way forward was negotiation. Polly learned that she must be firmer with her husband, much as his mother had been when he was a child. George discovered that his wife was responsive enough to abolish his "need" for tantrums. Fortunately, both the marriage and the pregnancy continued. Both Polly and George were proud and happy when the baby arrived. Polly never fully regained her sexual spontaneity after George's doubts about her, but their lovemaking was enjoyable and their relationship loving enough for her to want to continue having sex.

Although spontaneity was lacking for the post-partum Polly, their sex life was still intimate and highly pleasurable

CASE NOTES

GEORGE AND POLLY

The differences in attitude between George and Polly, and the consequent mistrust that entered their relationship, were due partly to their different family backgrounds and partly to the different cultures in which each was brought up.

Influences

The personality-forming effects of family and culture were very powerful and overlapping influences for George and Polly. Their effects, which had begun in early childhood, persisted throughout the couple's adult lives. As a result of them being from such differing backgrounds, their relationship was fraught with conflict and mutual misunderstanding, through no fault of either partner.

Differences

Almost every conflict can be resolved by negotiation, and that was the case with the differences between George and Polly. First, however, they needed to examine their own and each other's family backgrounds (see Family Constellations, page 32) and cultural influences (see page 56) to understand the effect that these had exerted upon their attitudes toward life and relationships. Having done this, each began to see exactly how the problem had arisen and to realize that, fundamentally, neither of them was really to blame. They also realized that their relationship was not doomed, as they had at first feared. By talking things through, they were able to overcome their differences and rebuild their relationship, which, in fact, was strengthened by having been tested almost to destruction.

BELIEF SYSTEMS

Just as we learn from our parents through spoken language, so too we learn through unspoken language, via sight, touch, and smell. A mother who glares at her daughter on finding her sitting on her boyfriend's knee is letting her know that she disapproves of this expression of sexuality. The daughter knows this because she has learned her values—her belief systems—from those who are closest to her, and her mother is possibly closest of all.

COMPATIBLE BELIEFS
The sense of familiarity that you can find with a lover can be a joyous discovery. It normally arises because he or she embodies something that you have found in your own family background, some behavior or belief that is the same as yours. This can calm anxieties and give you a sense of well-being and happiness. On the other hand, problems can occur when you and your lover have different patterns of belief.

Most young children learn that, if they feel afraid or hurt, a hug will make everything better, and that naughtiness may bring a frown or a scowl from a parent that will cause sadness. These unspoken messages reinforce the ideas about life placed in our minds from earliest childhood by direct and overheard comments and the actions of other family members.

THE GROWTH OF BELIEFS

Our immediate environment—the people in our families and the way they interact with one another—therefore becomes our "norm." Often it is through the unconscious absorption of our parents' standards that we gain our own. But this is not always a benefit. If a boy grows up in a family where his mother is the breadwinner and his father the homemaker, he may feel comfortable with homemaking himself in later life. If Dad hates women, however, that boy may unconsciously learn to do so, too.

Since each family is unique, it is reasonable to assume that each will have developed its own sets of attitudes and beliefs. Until quite recently, families were expected to remain within their particular social classes, and there was a firm belief that for a marriage to work, both partners should come from the same class because shared beliefs and world view would strengthen the union.

Making allowances for your partner's beliefs can help you understand how your partner views the world.

Nowadays, though, a general loosening of the class structure, combined with greater mobility and the rapid growth of technology, mean that we can no longer take anything about our partners for granted. So when, as adults, we form loving relationships, it is increasingly possible that we will do so with partners who come from different backgrounds and possess very different cultural and familial belief systems to our own.

SEXUAL HAPPINESS AND BELIEFS

When we fall in love, our beliefs meet up with those of our partners. One of the great discoveries we make when we fall in love is how wonderful it is to find someone with whom we feel we match. That sense of matching is a strong characteristic of the early stages of love, and it can feel utterly joyful and completing. And if we're lucky, our deeply rooted belief systems will interlock with those of our partners.

Many women who express their feelings in women's sexuality groups show that the kind of loving example parents set us in childhood directly affects how we respond sexually to our own partners in adult life. A child of a marriage between warm, openly loving parents will probably have few inhibitions during lovemaking, will respond freely and warmly to displays of affection, and will discover sexuality naturally and sensuously.

Children who are taught that their genitals are dirty may be inhibited in later sexual contact, and those taught to believe in rigid gender stereotypes may find perfectly natural behavior in their partners unattractive. One woman lost interest in her husband because he didn't always stand to urinate, and she saw this as effeminate and a turn-off. Talking openly but tactfully about such differences and not being afraid to try new things are ways of readapting and overcoming these problems.

When people reach adolescence they begin to apply their belief systems to close personal and sexual relationships. The degree of emotional and physical closeness in these relationships increases as the teenagers get older and their belief systems are molded by experience and peer attitudes. If a teenager's relationship with his or her parents is close, the parents' attitudes toward sexual encounters may have a great impact on the adolescent's. If that teenager is at odds with the parental views, however, sex may be used in rebellion. But each teenager will eventually choose how he or she will approach sex. For example, one may see sex as an expression of intimacy and affection, another as casual gratification.

TOO MUCH FOR HIM
Alan and Val had not been married for long when it became apparent that they had a problem— he did not share her firm belief that a lot of sex is an essential part of a happy relationship (see pages 52–55).

LEARNING TO ADAPT

When partners reconcile their belief system differences it is often surprising how much a few basic, if subtle, differences have affected them. In the case of Alan and Val (*see pages 52–55*), Val believed that constant physical relations were the basis of an enduring loving relationship. This made Alan feel overwhelmed and apprehensive about his performance. As a result, both worried that their mutual love was in jeopardy. Understanding each other's belief systems eased their problem.

MISMATCHED LIBIDOS

When you are at the beginning of what you hope will be a long-term sexual relationship, you expect to do a certain amount of compromising. But after only six months together, Val felt rejected because Alan didn't want as much sex as she did.

TOO MUCH OF A GOOD THING

There are many reasons why two people discover they have what appears to be a sexual mismatch. Differing libidos, where one partner is much more highly sexed than the other, is a common culprit, as is a high level of anxiety in one partner, who then finds reassurance in intercourse. A third cause, less common but nonetheless just as distressing, is when one partner believes that a lot of hot sex is the basis of a happy marriage and the other does not. Alan had no idea that this was what drove his new partner, Val, to demand such seemingly constant sex. All he did know was that he was expected to "perform" every night of the week—and twice on Sundays.

HURTFUL REJECTION

"I'm being deluged with sex," Alan explained. "When it's bedtime, Val is always there ahead of me, often dressed up in something exotic that I'm expected to rip off her. I thought all this was wonderful at first—I still think *she's* wonderful—but I feel as if I'm being forced. I'd like to be able to choose." Val, who had nothing but good intentions, was terribly hurt by Alan's attitude. "I feel so rejected when he says these things," she said.

Val devised inventive sex games in an attempt to increase Alan's enthusiasm

Alan enjoyed sex and was a capable lover, but too much of it bored him

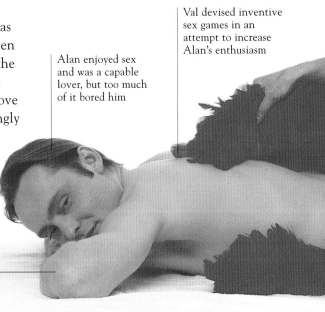

Val's constant demands were beginning to take their toll on Alan's vitality

WONDERFUL SEX, WONDERFUL LIFE

"For me, a loving relationship is about caring for my man and doing everything to make him feel wonderful," said Val. "I want him to be really happy and secure so that he feels that everything is all right for him in the world. I certainly thought that having a wonderful sex life was a good way of doing this."

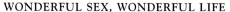

Val enjoyed sex, but valued it more as an expression of Alan's love for her than as a source of pleasure

ALIENATION

The differences in sexual expectations alienated the couple from each other. "When he'd rather read than make love," said Val, "it feels as if something is wrong— with me." She believed their love was fading because of the tension between them.

Sharing the Initiative

When a loving couple finds that sex has become a domestic struggle, it's vital that both partners consider all possible reasons for this. On the surface, Val simply wanted too much sex. But why? Was she just highly sexed, or was the answer more complicated?

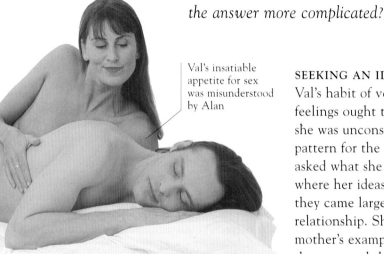

Val's insatiable appetite for sex was misunderstood by Alan

SEEKING AN IDEAL

Val's habit of voicing what she thought Alan's feelings ought to be was a clue. It seemed that she was unconsciously following some kind of pattern for the "ideal" relationship. When asked what she thought this ideal might be, and where her ideas came from, she admitted that they came largely from memories of her parents' relationship. She felt that by following her mother's example of constant generous giving, she expected the same security that there had been in her own family.

ENDURING LOVE

Despite the difficulties caused by their differing approach to lovemaking, Alan and Val were still very much in love and were desperate to find some form of solution to their problems. For this reason they were both willing to open up about their childhood family lives.

RECONCILING DIFFERENCES

In Alan's family, giving pleasure hadn't been solely a woman's responsibility, and he found it hard to understand Val's position. Once he understood that she believed the success of their relationship was threatened, he did everything he could to reassure her.

CASE NOTES

VAL AND ALAN

The apparent sexual incompatibility between Val and Alan was not physical in origin but a conflict of beliefs. Val believed the key to a happy relationship was generosity and giving to your partner, including plenty of sex. Alan, however, enjoyed sex but didn't share Val's belief that the more sex a couple has, the happier they'll be. He preferred quality to quantity.

Overcoming differences

The attitudes each of them had about the role of sex within a relationship were aspects of their overall beliefs about how partners should treat each other. Because these beliefs had been instilled in each of them in childhood, it would not be easy for either partner to change them. Compromise appeared to be the fairest and most effective solution.

Val and Alan began with the "I Should" exercise (see page 84) to analyze their respective beliefs and identify their similarities and differences. They then used this information to work out a reconciliation. The compromise they agreed was a "sex contract" to balance between Val's needs and Alan's wants.

SEX CONTRACT

Comparing the beliefs that they'd gained from their families gave them the mutual insight to see that the solution was a sex contract. Each partner would have three nights a week on which to decide whether or not to have sex, the seventh being optional. This would give both a choice of action. Alan could also find nonsexual ways to ease Val's sense of rejection.

ACTION PLAN

 IF YOU HAVE *relationship difficulties that arise from differing belief systems, analyze your character to see how it affects the way you think about the world, and* ask your partner to analyze his or hers, too. Then both look back *at your cultural influences to see why your attitudes have grown the way they have. This will help both of you to see more clearly the best ways to progress and strengthen your relationship.*

ESTABLISHING YOUR PERSONALITY TYPE

According to the therapist H. H. Mosak, most personality types derive their characteristics from priorities they unconsciously decided on in early childhood. Although it's possible to have more than one personality priority, there's usually a dominant one. If you can, pinpoint your personality type, but if this is difficult, ask your partner to help (he or she should be objective and factual).

Mosak says there are certain easily recognizable types. One way to establish your most likely priority is to see which of those listed below are most relevant and then whittle these down to one.

- *The Getters, who exploit and manipulate life and others.*
- *The Drivers, who are overly ambitious and dedicated.*
- *The Aginners, who oppose all life's expectations and demands and who rarely know what they are for but always what they are against.*

- *The Victims, who embrace disaster and elicit the sympathy and pity of others.*
- *The Martyrs, who either silently endure or make their suffering highly visible.*
- *The Babies, who exploit others with charm and cuteness.*
- *The Inadequates, who do nothing correctly and constantly need help.*
- *The Intellectualizers and Rationalizers, who place a barrier of thought between themselves and their feelings.*

If you and your partner can each identify what your personal priorities are, you can then work out whether they are in conflict in any way. If they are, you should try to maximize the advantages and minimize the disadvantages that arise from this conflict. Building on each other's emotional and psychological strengths, and making allowances for any weaknesses, will help you make your relationship happier and closer.

CULTURAL INFLUENCES

It is important to understand the influence of your culture on the formation of your beliefs to help you evaluate them and put them into context. To understand the origins of your beliefs, think back to how the outside world, the people and places that immediately surrounded you, appeared to you when you were a child. Then answer these questions:

- *Can you think of five beliefs that you had about the outside world? For example, did you believe that it was hostile, or friendly?*
- *Do any of those early beliefs match your current views about the world? If so, which ones?*
- *Where do you think those early beliefs came from? From within you, or from a relation, or from some other source, such as books or television?*
- *Are any of those beliefs outdated?*
- *How does the reality of the outside world compare with the way you would like it to be?*
- *Is there a way you might gain this ideal world? Are there changes you could make to assist this?*

Ask your partner to examine the origins of his or her beliefs in the same way, and then compare your findings. This will help you explore the background behind each other's beliefs, and so gain greater understanding of each other.

LEARN TO COMMUNICATE

Do you listen properly when your partner talks to you? Do you know if your partner really listens to you? Communication skills are easy to learn and easy to use, and the rewards speak for themselves.

THE ROLE OF COMMUNICATION

Undoubtedly, communication is at the root of good feelings in a relationship and, unfortunately, also at the root of bad. But we communicate in so many ways, some of which we may not be fully aware of, that it can be difficult for other people, including our partners, to understand exactly what it is that we are trying to tell them.

One of the most important roles of a counselor—regardless of the type of counseling he or she is offering—is to teach people how to communicate. This is because, alas, some people don't even know how to have a real conversation. Indeed, one of the main reasons that many relationships deteriorate is the way in which the partners converse.

CONVERSATION STRUCTURE

Conversations—good ones, that is—have a structure. This consists of talking (*see page 60*), listening, negotiating, and taking action. If you can use this structure correctly, many difficulties can be resolved and the core of your love improves. You get to experience warm feelings toward each other again—a kind of emotional renewal—or put an end to a relationship once and for all. The latter is not always so bad, because it lets you know where you stand and frees you to make a new start.

This chapter of the book analyzes the separate stages of a conversation, and describes ways in which you and your partner can improve the quality of your conversations. It also gives examples of conversations that work, examples of using negotiation, and simple exercises to help you take action once a compromise has been reached.

RESPECT AND RESPONSIBILITY

This chapter also discusses the issues of mutual respect and responsibility. It is invariably through the use of language that respect is demonstrated (as, of course, is disrespect). What is interesting is that men and women often speak disrespectfully when they don't mean to. Even though a man or woman respects his or her lover, it seems all too easy to lapse into speech patterns, learned as children, which put the other down. Gaining awareness of bad habits, and using the "May I?" exercise *(see page 84)* will help you to overcome such behavior.

When a partner feels anxious about whether or not he or she is in control, a situation of overcontrol tends to develop. This mistake usually occurs when one partner is not allowing the other to have responsibility for areas of his or her life. It is important, therefore, to accord a partner's responsibilities to that partner and to allow each individual that much-needed "space" and that all-important respect.

LISTENING

Many people dismiss listening as being so passive that it doesn't count as an area in which you can take positive action. Good listening is far from passive, however, and consists of giving important signals and responses *(see page 66)*. One thing that maddens most people during a conversation is when they've made a particularly impassioned statement and, instead of acknowledging what they've said, the listener replies with something seemingly unconnected. This feels frustrating and devaluing, but usually it is not the case that what was said was unworthy of a response. It is more likely to be that the listener is poor at giving feedback.

NEGOTIATING

If your conversation is actually an argument or a heated squabble over a tricky issue, it should also contain negotiation *(see page 72)*, and any true negotiation must include compromise. When two people have opposing views they may not necessarily be reconciled, but concessions can be made on both sides. Although this often means that neither of you will be entirely happy with the outcome, the fact that you have resolved the situation will give reassurance to both of you.

TAKING ACTION

Talking about compromise is fine, but if no action is taken, then the discussion is worthless. One of the toughest aspects of promises made while compromising is the need to carry them out *(see page 78)*. Nothing is worse than being let down by a partner, so you must be able and willing to fulfill any promises you make.

BENEFITS OF COMMUNICATION
Achieving a level of communication that works in a relationship involves hard work on both sides—but the gains are well worth it.

TALKING

A loving relationship, particularly a healthy marriage, should be a partnership between equals. If so, each partner will feel relaxed in the other's company and won't feel the need to struggle against the other's personality. Unfortunately, this isn't always easy. If one partner feels inadequate or lacking in skills, he or she may feel the need to compensate for this with aggression or spite.

MUTUAL ANTAGONISM

RETALIATION

SPEAKER — Verbal Attack → LISTENER

NO RETALIATION

ANTAGONISM DECLINES

VERBAL ATTACK AND RETALIATION
Repeated retaliation to verbal attacks can lead to rising levels of mutual antagonism. Consciously avoiding retaliation will help defuse the situation.

Any difference in intensity of feeling between partners may be due, in part, to either partner's upbringing. In the attempt to feel good about him- or herself, and equal to his or her partner, one may inadvertently cause the other to feel bad. This in turn may lead to whoever is on the receiving end taking some sort of defensive or retaliatory action, scoring off the first partner and again making him or her feel inferior. Such seesawing ultimately causes unhappiness.

WHAT CAN BE DONE?

The basis of improving your relationship is to talk in special ways. Once you learn, or relearn, how to talk to one another, the core of your love improves. Cast your mind back over the early months of your relationship, when the conversation was happy and encouraging. Now see what there is today. Perhaps you tell each other less often that "You're looking good," or give little encouragement when it's asked of you? Maybe you sense that you are marking time emotionally, and so is your partner.

There may be many reasons why your conversations have changed from positive to negative. But one of the main causes of dissatisfaction can be the way you talk to each other. If one partner feels slighted or put down, the self-defense mechanism comes into play in the form of further slights, which prolongs the battle for superiority. All this points to the fact that if you want to start feeling better you have to help your partner feel better too. But where to begin?

FIRST PRINCIPLES

It is amazing how tongue-tied men and women become when they settle into a long-term relationship. The simplest, yet most important phrase, "I love you," becomes terribly hard to say. More people should practice the homework of saying "I love you" at least three times a week, and try in any way they can to reinforce the words with actions. This will serve to make a partner feel special and secure within the relationship. It is also important that people set aside time to talk. Voicing feelings when your partner is exhausted after work, watching television, or is in the middle of cooking will not help communication. Indeed, it may make your partner less responsive and more irritable than usual, causing him or her to overlook the importance of the words.

VERBAL BULLYING

Assuming you still feel respect for your partner, consider why you are not showing it in the way you speak to him or her. After all, if you feel that your partner is truly your equal, then surely you should respect his or her feelings. Perhaps you constantly tell your partner what to do, or how to do it. Have you considered that your helpful advice could come across as constant criticism? Don't stop offering help, but consider *how* you offer it.

It may be that in your attempt to feel in control you begin to talk down to your partner, treating him or her like a child, or even like an inferior. It is very difficult for someone, treated as an inferior, to respond as an equal. You must allow people to take responsibility for themselves.

Another way of showing respect for your partner is to allow him or her to speak freely. It's quite common for one partner to get into the habit of answering for the other one, or even of finishing the other's sentences. This kind of talking is a "mistaken method" by which the talker gets to feel in control. It can cause the second partner to feel invisible, sometimes to the extent of feeling incapable of answering honestly and fully. Making a conscious decision to hold your tongue, even if your partner is struggling, can boost his or her self-confidence.

If a person is on the receiving end of such treatment, it may help if he or she consciously interrupts by holding up a hand and saying "Stop!" He or she could then ask, "May I have permission to speak now?" and keep asking until the answer is "Yes." If this doesn't work, he or she could hold up an object, car keys, for example, as a signal that silence must be maintained for as long as these are held (*see page 84*).

SILENCE

This is often employed as a method of avoiding any issue that feels dangerous. For a partner to talk openly or to confide, he or she needs reassurance that discussing certain topics will not lead to emotional confrontation. It is very important that if such reassurances are given they are carefully adhered to and confrontation avoided. Once such trust has been broken it is very difficult to regain. No empty promises here.

CHILDHOOD LESSONS
A partner who constantly dominates a conversation may well be employing a defense mechanism that stems from childhood—in large families, it often happens that if you don't talk all the time, you don't get heard. This was the case with Julio, who could talk but would not listen, and endangered his marriage by rarely letting his wife, Maria, get a word in edgewise (see pages 62–65).

CONSTANT INTERRUPTION

Some people simply cannot resist speaking on behalf of their partners. Julio not only did this in the consulting room when he came for counseling help, he even did it at home, in bed! As a result, his wife, Maria, had finally gone on strike.

When Maria held the keys, Julio had to let her speak

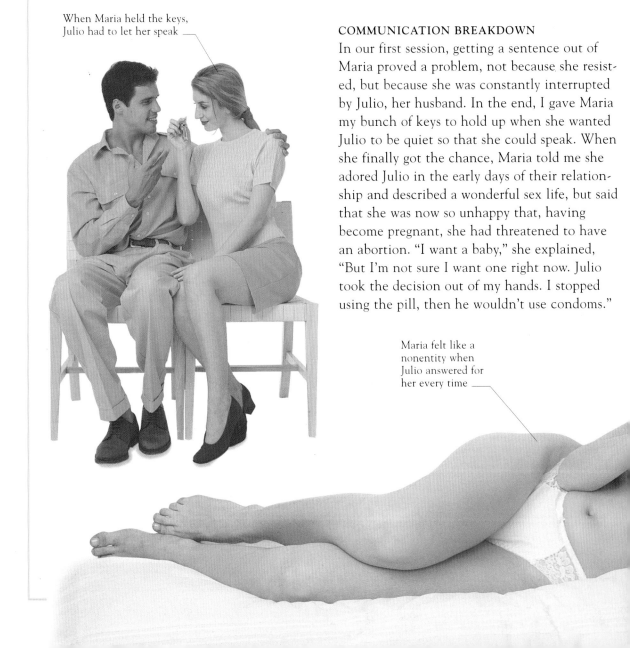

Maria felt like a nonentity when Julio answered for her every time

COMMUNICATION BREAKDOWN

In our first session, getting a sentence out of Maria proved a problem, not because she resisted, but because she was constantly interrupted by Julio, her husband. In the end, I gave Maria my bunch of keys to hold up when she wanted Julio to be quiet so that she could speak. When she finally got the chance, Maria told me she adored Julio in the early days of their relationship and described a wonderful sex life, but said that she was now so unhappy that, having become pregnant, she had threatened to have an abortion. "I want a baby," she explained, "But I'm not sure I want one right now. Julio took the decision out of my hands. I stopped using the pill, then he wouldn't use condoms."

Verbal bullying or domination drives lovers apart

ANGER

Maria complained that it was very difficult for her to explain herself to Julio when he was always speaking for her, and became very embarrassed when she described how their sex life had ground to a halt. "It's not that I don't find him attractive," she said, "But I'm so angry I can't let myself get near him."

CASE NOTES

MARIA AND JULIO

Julio found it very hard at first to remember to allow Maria the chance to speak. Fortunately, his love for Maria prompted a concerted effort on his part.

Conversation etiquette
Using two of the exercises on page 84, the "May I?" and the Holder of the Keys, the couple began to address the imbalance in their communication. The former exercise, which involved Julio consciously saying "May I?" at the beginning of a conversation, was particularly helpful because it forced him to consider his words before speaking. It also gave Maria the opportunity to refuse his verbal advances.

Using the Holder of the Keys exercise meant that Maria had a tool for keeping Julio quiet—in this case, holding a ring of keys. This let Maria establish control over their conversations, and the freedom she then felt helped her overcome her anger with Julio and settle once more into a loving relationship.

LIFE CHANGES

"Sometimes, I find myself flinching even when he only wants to hold my hand," she revealed. "I depend on my friends, as Julio is often away, and when he's home he talks so hard, he barely notices me. He even answers for me in bed." He'd ask her something and then give the reply. Maria doubted the wisdom of parenthood under such circumstances.

Taking Turns

When she was given the chance to speak, Maria was able to voice her fears about Julio. Although it was initially painful for both of them, this openness and the truths it revealed allowed them to reinforce their feelings for each other as Maria's words directly affected Julio's actions.

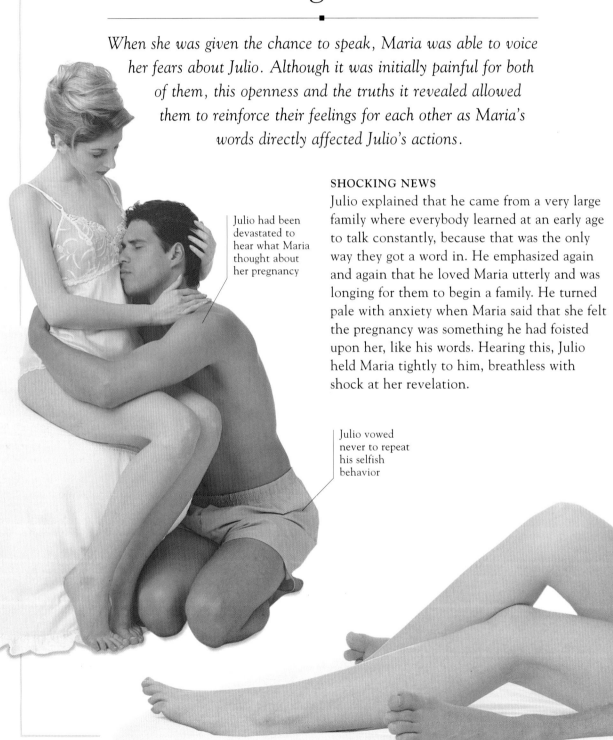

Julio had been devastated to hear what Maria thought about her pregnancy

Julio vowed never to repeat his selfish behavior

SHOCKING NEWS

Julio explained that he came from a very large family where everybody learned at an early age to talk constantly, because that was the only way they got a word in. He emphasized again and again that he loved Maria utterly and was longing for them to begin a family. He turned pale with anxiety when Maria said that she felt the pregnancy was something he had foisted upon her, like his words. Hearing this, Julio held Maria tightly to him, breathless with shock at her revelation.

TIME TO SPEAK

During counseling, use of the Holder of the
Keys technique *(see page 84)* proved invaluable
as a means of deterring Julio from interrupting
Maria and of giving her time to speak. This was
necessary because she thought carefully about

what she was going to
say, but tended to
gather her thoughts
rather slowly. They
were, however, intelli-
gent thoughts that
deserved to be heard.

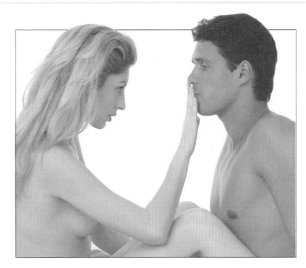

CHANGE OF APPROACH

Alarmed by the damage he'd inflicted, Julio
made a concerted effort to change his
approach to his wife. He also changed the
hours he worked, starting earlier each
morning so that he got back home earlier.
Maria, in turn, made some new friends.
Although no deliberate decision
was made, when Maria realized
how much effort Julio was
putting into making
changes in his behavior,
she felt greatly relieved—
so much so that her
pregnancy at last became
a pleasure for her.

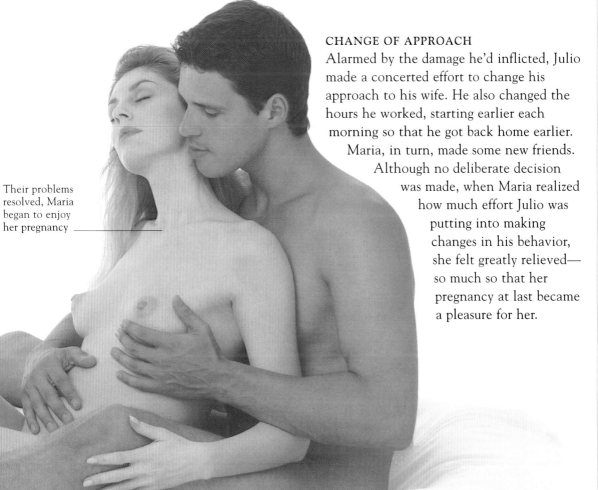

Their problems
resolved, Maria
began to enjoy
her pregnancy

LISTENING

Like talking, listening is a major ingredient of proper communication. To be a good listener you need to appreciate that listening does not just mean hearing words—it involves concentrating on the speaker and on what he or she is saying, indicating verbally and with body language that you are listening, and encouraging the speaker to continue.

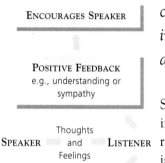

ENCOURAGES SPEAKER

POSITIVE FEEDBACK
e.g., understanding or sympathy

SPEAKER — Thoughts and Feelings — LISTENER

NEGATIVE FEEDBACK
e.g., indifference or hostility

DISCOURAGES SPEAKER

LISTENER FEEDBACK
Reactions to a speaker's words can have powerful effects. Negative feedback is discouraging; positive supports and encourages.

Some of the most unsatisfactory conversations are those one-sided affairs in which one partner is not listening to what the other is saying, and refuses to look the other in the eyes or even to acknowledge that he or she is talking. This type of behavior is almost guaranteed to infuriate, because the inattentive partner is ignoring the key ingredients of good listening: concentration and good feedback.

CONCENTRATION

In order to show clearly that you are listening, you do actually have to listen. This means that concentration is vital. If you let your mind wander, you are wasting both your partner's time and your own. One of the most effective aids to good listening is to put your own feelings and thoughts on hold for a while. Concentrating on your partner's face when he or she speaks does not mean that you should stare intimidatingly, but if you drop your gaze for too long, your partner may feel that he or she has lost your attention. The art is to maintain the correct degree of eye contact, which often comes naturally if you are interested in the speaker. If your partner needs to talk, give him or her your undivided attention. If you are watching TV, or listening to the radio, switch it off. If you are reading, put the book aside and do not play with it while your partner is talking. Fiddling with the pages will only give the impression that you find the conversation an unwanted interruption. Try to sit opposite your partner, at equal heights if possible, so that you both feel that you are communicating on equal terms. Sit in an open posture—don't fold your arms across your chest, for example—and try to ensure that you are not having to twist around to face your partner nor that you have any physical barrier such as furniture between you.

Good listening is an essential part of good communication and is an art that is well worth learning.

Timing is also important. It can be very difficult not to be tempted to postpone the conversation until *you* feel like talking. For this reason, both of you should try not to leave discussions until bedtime, and particularly not until you are actually in bed, when the need for sleep can be used as an excuse to avoid a discussion. It is also all too easy to get the wrong impressions and misinterpret each other if you are both lying in the dark.

GIVING FEEDBACK

The most difficult conversations are those with people whose facial expressions and body language give no hint as to their feelings on what you are saying. It can be terribly off-putting when the person with whom you are trying to communicate—especially if it is your partner—shows absolutely no sign of registering your words, or even of having heard you. To ensure that this does not happen to your partner when he or she is speaking, let your face register your feelings and encourage your partner with a nod or words of agreement.

It is very important that your partner have a chance to say everything that he or she needs to. This is his or her platform and you must not interrupt, no matter how unfair you think the version of events may be. You will get your chance later. If you feel that you absolutely must comment on a point that has been raised, note it down and bring it up again later. People often begin with small, niggling aggravations and build up to the true problem, so if you counter every point raised you may well waste valuable time on things that really aren't that important to either of you, and fail to reach the crux of the matter.

The final feedback is to make sure that you understand exactly what your partner has been saying before you discuss it. Repeat back to him or her a brief description of what you think has been said and, if you are wrong, allow your partner to clarify any confusing points or give more details.

PROBLEMS

Don't dismiss a partner's gripe for any reason. You are different people and will both think and feel differently about many things. Another's point of view is just as valid as yours. If you have feelings left from childhood that make you feel as if your partner's feelings are somehow an attack on you, aimed at proving you wrong or inferior, think again. It is vital to remember that your partner is an individual and that his or her need to express deep feelings does not negate the fact that he or she cares for you. Listening isn't a passive process!

COMMUNICATION
BREAKDOWN
The breakdown in communication that happens when one partner ceases to listen to the other can often put an intolerable strain on a relationship, as Ronnie and Claire discovered (see pages 68–71).

ONE-SIDED CONVERSATIONS

*It can be hurtful when your partner won't listen to what you say,
especially when all you are asking for is something as simple as
a kiss on the lips. When that happened repeatedly to Claire, she
began to suspect that it was a symptom of a deeper problem.*

THE NEED FOR A KISS

For some people, a kiss on the lips connects directly to their
sexual response system. Claire was unhappy because her
husband, Ronnie, was denying her this sensuous experience.
Claire said that before their marriage Ronnie had lavished
kisses on her. "In the days before we had intercourse, he'd kiss
me on the lips till I was dizzy
with arousal. But since
then, the kissing has
stopped. He'll kiss
my neck, but it's
not the same."

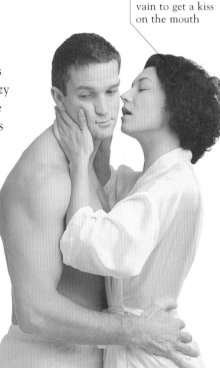

Claire tried in
vain to get a kiss
on the mouth

Ronnie seemed
willing to kiss
Claire anywhere
but on the lips

CHANGE OF HEART

"Now we make love less often and I'm rarely
satisfied," Claire continued. "I always ask him
to kiss me more during lovemaking but he just
ignores me. Then I get angry. It's so sad. I'm
very attached to him." Understanding
Ronnie's change of heart was difficult—there
seemed little wrong between man and wife.

DENIAL

"I'm here reluctantly," Ronnie admitted. "Claire is always making a fuss—a mountain out of a molehill. Our lovemaking is fine; there's no problem. If Claire finds it hard to climax, I satisfy her by hand. I seem to be surrounded by hysterical women. If it's not Claire sounding off, it's her sister or my mother."

Giving Ronnie a massage made Claire feel more intimate with him

INCREASING INTIMACY WITH MASSAGE

When people deny there's a problem, it's usually because they are terrified of facing that problem. In many instances, people like Ronnie need to be given special reassurance before they will open up. Claire considered when Ronnie felt most secure in the relationship and decided that it was when she was doing things especially for him—such as giving him a deep muscle massage. She was aware that it would be good if she could do more of this.

A deep muscle massage made Ronnie feel more relaxed

Learning to Listen

By acknowledging that he was mistaken in his idea that Claire was making a lot of fuss about nothing, and by learning to listen to what she had to say, Ronnie rediscovered how much he really loved her and how good she made him feel. Their sex life—and their relationship as a whole—was soon on the mend.

DIFFICULT MOTHER

Ronnie's apparent inability to demonstrate warmth mainly related to his relationship with his mother, a difficult woman who constantly demanded his attention and never listened to him. The irony was that he was now subjecting his wife to the same treatment. When Claire asked Ronnie to kiss her, he refused, causing her to burst into tears. But when he realized he was seeing his wife as an attention-grabber like his mother, it was a breakthrough.

REALIZING WHAT YOU'VE GOT

Although the two were very different, Ronnie had confused Claire with his mother. But when he listed all the positive aspects about her, she voiced some very appreciative remarks in return. For this, he surprised her with a kiss.

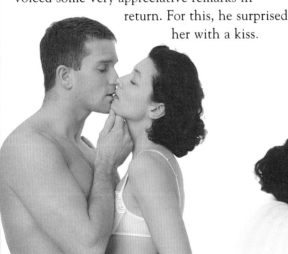

Ronnie was now more than happy to kiss Claire wherever she wanted

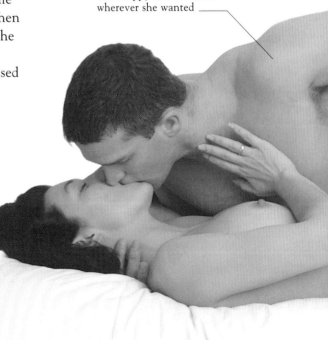

LEARNING COMMUNICATION

The key to improving Ronnie's deep-seated problem with listening was the Three-Stage Communication exercise *(see page 84)*. Using this, he and Claire could be sure that when either spoke the other truly listened to what was being said.

PERFECT PROGRESS

Some months later, with hard work and the help of this exercise, the atmosphere between the couple was far warmer. Ronnie no longer saw Claire as overly demanding, they were making love again, and Claire was getting her kisses!

CASE NOTES

RONNIE AND CLAIRE

Ronnie and Claire needed to deal with a backlog of rejection that hinged on Ronnie's belief that nothing was wrong and that Claire was merely "sounding off." But once he realized that his wife truly heard what he was saying, Ronnie's love life improved. Claire's feelings that her husband no longer wanted to be intimate with her were very difficult for her to face. For this reason it was a relief for her to discover that the source of the problem lay elsewhere.

For Ronnie, the difficulties he had faced in communicating with his mother had widened (in his mind) to encompass all the women in his family—his wife, her sister, and his mother.

Communication exercises

By practicing the Three-Stage Communication exercise (see page 84), Ronnie and Claire were able to reestablish good listening in their marriage. This exercise taught Ronnie how to listen to Claire's words and respond to them in a positive way rather than to grow irritated by the fact that she was talking. Through this he could once again show Claire the respect she required and fulfill her unmet physical need, which was to be kissed.

Claire, on the other hand, began to feel that her words were penetrating her husband's mind, and that he actually understood what she was saying.

NEGOTIATING

In any conversation there need to be good talkers and good listeners. This situation changes when a conversation evolves into a discussion, for there may be a point where either an agreement, or at least an understanding, must be reached by all concerned. If the subject of a discussion is as personal as intimate feelings, it is important that both parties understand how to negotiate.

Often, truly satisfying talks are those that contain an element of learning. The joint exploration of an idea can sometimes result in an exhilarating realization that a new understanding has been achieved. Even if the conversations are about completely mundane subjects, it doesn't matter—it is the matching of minds that is so wonderful. Unfortunately, the chances are that five years into a relationship, or ten, or twenty, couples will have settled into habits that, while still comfortable and reassuring, are also dull. Too often this affects how partners talk to each other, in many cases because each sticks to patterns of talk that he or she has grown accustomed to. This can cause problems when they try to resolve a disagreement.

In order to make progress in your relationship it is important that you learn the give and take of negotiation.

COMMUNICATING FEELINGS

It is common for one or both partners in a relationship to allow negative emotions, such as frustration, disappointment, or anger, to affect their trust, caring, and respect for a partner. For many people, a momentary outburst can cause a conversation to turn into a fight. In the heat of the moment it is very easy to forget how to communicate in a positive way. It is therefore vital to take a step back and concentrate on your true feelings.

THE VALUE OF COMPROMISE

In the earliest days of a love affair, even your disagreements may be exhilarating. You probably felt independent enough to concede differences without feeling personally threatened, which may have helped you to voice your own feelings freely and get to know your partner even more intimately. You were able to listen to the very different ideas of your partner with an open mind, and maybe you even changed as a result. You may

WORKING TOGETHER
When you decide to work toward a solution, it does not mean that one partner concedes that the other is right. This will simply place that partner in the wrong, making him or her more likely to feel the need to fight back on another occasion. Both partners need to accept that changes are needed on both sides.

have compromised your views and patterns of behavior because the prize of your partner's love made this feel practical and sensible. All this may mean that you lived together very comfortably—in the beginning.

Sadly, one of the great dilemmas of closeness to another person, especially one you love dearly, is that the closeness itself can feel threatening. It is the great paradox of love: the person we adore may also be the person we feel we must resist. This leads to problems and, in self-defense, we close our minds to compromise—and the battles begin.

SHARING AND LEARNING

In a disagreement, the roles of speaker and listener still apply but the dialogue fails to move on to sharing and learning, at least not in the way you may have been used to. In order to progress from this unproductive situation, the extra elements of negotiation and compromise must be used. There is no point in going through the pain of talking about a difficulty if a working solution isn't proposed. Fights may be cathartic but, unless problems are dealt with, there will only be a lull before the next storm.

REALISTIC AGREEMENTS

There is no point, once you are in agreement, in making unrealistic suggestions, promises, or demands. Working solutions mean conceding certain aspects without agreeing to anything that feels wrong to you.

Take, for instance, a man whose partner is feeling jealous, insecure, and excluded from his life. It would be easy for him to say that he will include her completely in his life, but almost impossible to carry out. For this reason he should make his concessions practicable. He should acknowledge that he takes his partner's anxieties seriously and propose changes in his own behavior that will ease her fears.

While stating that he will still maintain friendships outside the marriage, he could agree to spend more time together and make a concerted effort to show how he feels about her. Thus he will maintain his independence and boost her confidence.

WILLING NEGOTIATION

One positive use of negotiation is to include an aspect of understanding in your complaint. Any ground given must not be seen as a token gesture. Negotiation should show a willingness to reach a true compromise—not that this should negate the importance of the complaint. If you back down before you've even begun, why complain in the first place?

GIVE TO GET
Both compromise and negotiation are based on the give-to-get principle. If you go some way to meeting your partner's needs, doubtless he or she will feel warmer and more loving about your needs. By offering a little you will create an upward spiral of improved feeling.

TIME OFF FROM SEX
Diana (see pages 74–77) found herself having to negotiate with her husband, Brian, for time off from lovemaking when she was studying for her exams.

TIME OFF FROM SEX

When we're young we need to live life quickly. If, for whatever reason, a partner denies us sex, it can feel impossible to last without it. Even though Brian knew Diana would have time for him at a later date, he insisted he couldn't cope with her refusal now.

NO CONCENTRATION

Brian and Diana, who had previously had problems with their mismatched sexual expectations (*see pages 22–25*), returned to therapy with a new problem. Diana had returned to college as a mature student, and was feeling anxious about her forthcoming exams—examination time is notorious for bad temper, anxiety attacks, depression, and obsessions. She and Brian had been enjoying an enthusiastic sex life, but suddenly this had stopped and Diana had lost interest. "I just can't concentrate with Brian around me," she explained.

I recommended that each of them try self-pleasuring and fantasizing

Diana's preoccupation with her exams made her lose interest in sex

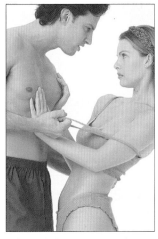

ANGER

"I've got to pass these exams and they're only eight weeks away, but Brian's being an idiot," said Diana. "Sex is great but his temper is awful. In the past, anger turned us on. We've had some of our best lovemaking when fighting. But this is serious." Brian didn't understand, and denied Diana's accusations. "She is so rejecting. To need an eight-week break is either obsessive or she's telling me something I'd rather not know."

SELF-STIMULATION

Discovering the exact source of the problem, was vital to their relationship, but because of Diana's deadline, any counseling was going to have to be fast. For Diana, exams were the obvious cause. But what about her husband? To ease some of the sexual pressure the couple practiced stimulating themselves, in private, and tried fantasizing about each other.

CASE NOTES

BRIAN AND DIANA

For Diana, avoiding sex was a way for her to maintain a calm attitude to a very stressful time. She seemed to have perfectly rational reasons for cooling the physical side of her relationship with Brian. Her husband, however, saw her coolness as something far more sinister. A powerful emotional barrier had arisen between them, and it could be broken down only when they realized that the meaning of sex had become confused between them and agreed to compromise (see page 84).

When Diana offered a compromise, loving kisses and cuddles but no sex, Brian was quickly able to come to terms with the situation and see Diana's situation far more rationally and sympathetically.

Sex-free but loving intimacy filled the gap caused by Diana's revision and encouraged them both to relish their eventual return to sex.

The Hot and Cold exercise

Diana's coolness toward him made Brian feel rejected and vulnerable and caused him to retaliate with anger. It was very important therefore that Brian realize the negative effect his temper tantrums were having on the relationship. The Hot and Cold exercise (see page 84) can be used to see just how extreme your feelings of anger and distance, or warmth and closeness, are for your partner, and vice versa. This exercise gave Brian a powerful illustration of the damaging emotional effects of his anger, which had made him feel so cold and resentful toward his wife.

Agreeing on a Compromise

The lull that masturbation and fantasizing brought about for Brian and Diana meant that they were then able to approach the negotiations about their deadlock with calm rationality. This made it easier for them to reach a compromise that each was able to agree on and stick to.

Brian responded to the results of the Hot and Cold exercise with heartfelt feelings

BREAKING THE DEADLOCK

Brian was acutely anxious that the problem may have caused a permanent rift between him and Diana. To combat this the couple had to break the deadlock by learning how to negotiate, and how to acknowledge each other's fears. Dealing with Brian's fears first, Diana conceded to some loving hugs and kisses, even if sex was still out of the question.

COMPROMISE

Next, Brian had to realize that in order to get something, it helps to give. With difficulty, he agreed to Diana's "no intercourse" contract. The idea of compromise was new to him so the Hot and Cold exercise *(see page 84)* helped him see how much he was achieving. When it demonstrated how angry Brian was, he had the grace to be ashamed. He moved over to Diana, and hugged her.

When her exams were over, Diana's enthusiasm for lovemaking returned immediately

SELF-DISCIPLINE

The couple was encouraged by the idea of celebrating the end of Diana's exams with a special sexual treat. They were going to view the eight-week buildup to it as a kind of Tantric self-discipline—a delaying of gratification to make its eventual achievement all the more exciting.

LOOKING TO THE FUTURE

By postponing sexual release, Brian and Diana were likely to value lovemaking more when the time came again. For Brian this would be particularly gratifying as he would truly savor the experience. For Diana the release would be two-fold—sexually and in terms of her exams—and therefore her feelings for Brian would carry extra weight. The couple's eventual lovemaking would mark a new chapter in their life together.

TAKING ACTION

When you have discussed a problem with your partner and negotiated a solution, you must then be prepared to carry out any actions that you have agreed to even if you have second thoughts. That is why it is vital that you don't promise the impossible; a compromise is far better, because it proposes the possible. Even if you don't feel 100 percent in favor, there should be enough in your agreement for you to act on.

The consequences of not acting can be severe. If you draw back, time after time, you eventually lose your partner and feel great pain. For your partner, being let down again and again by the very person who is supposed to care above all others is an awful feeling. It will change how your partner sees you. Instead of adoring you, he or she will view you as weak or deceptive or outrageously selfish and will lose respect for you.

CARRYING OUT PROMISES

So how can you ensure that you carry out your promises? First, you have to be careful about how much you promise. Don't overextend yourself or you may end up disappointing both yourself and your partner. Then you should act methodically. Always write your agreements down in your diary so that you can build them into your day and it will be hard for them to slip your mind. In this way, if baby-sitting is part of your deal, note the baby-sitting nights in your diary and never suddenly or unthinkingly replace them with work or pleasure. If you are reorganizing the house so you can work at home, make a space in your diary for moving furniture and calling the phone company for an extra line so your partner faces as little disruption as possible.

Offering some real change is often necessary to convince your partner of your good intentions.

ASSERTIVENESS

If you find that you just can't take the necessary action, try dealing with it in a progressive manner. Use the Yes/No exercise to sort out your priorities. Over the period of a week, say "Yes" to three things you really want to do and "No" to three things you don't. These things can be banal or earth-shattering, but the exercise will help to clarify your priorities.

For example, if you are supposed to be coming straight home after work on Friday nights instead of going to the bar for a few drinks, you might like to ask yourself the following questions. Are you going to say "Yes" to coming home? Or are you going to say "No"? (You should say "Yes" to what you really want to do and "No" to what you really don't want to do.)

You may say "Yes" to coming home, because you know that if you don't, home won't be there much longer. In this case you are saying "Yes" to your long-term welfare. If you say "No," this may be because you feel better out at the bar and think that this counts more. In some cases, the "betterness" might tell us something about the emptiness of your marriage. Thus your "No" to going straight home has brought your real priority into focus.

There may be another aspect to this particular example, however, which is that perhaps alcohol is playing a big part in what is going wrong. In this event, you must get help with your drinking problem. Without help, everything you hold dear may be lost—it's as dramatic as that.

POSITIVE STEPS

Alcohol addiction aside, the Yes/No exercise may help you to work out that the problem is deeper than you suspected. If this is the case, it will mean going back to the negotiating table and saying unashamedly, "I've promised more than I can deliver. I'm sorry, but can we look at this again?" You are not—emphatically not—saying you won't or can't make moves to improve things. But you need to get back to negotiating.

In this event, the idea of a staggered contract is helpful. Try listing the changes you feel each should make. Then number these in order of difficulty. Starting with the least difficult, work your way through the list. By all means celebrate your successes but do not be afraid or ashamed to go back a step if you experience a failure. As you begin to achieve your goals you will feel stronger and more confident about future promises.

SAYING SORRY

Contrary to how things were when we were children, simply saying sorry is no longer enough when we are adults. Offering real change is what is necessary to convince your partner of your good intentions—remember that everyone has a breaking point. If you are persistently unfaithful, for example, there will come a time when your apologies won't work. You'll have blown it. So get in touch with the fact that childhood rules no longer apply. You're in the grown-up world now. The up side to all this hard work is that, even if the discomfort of tough words upsets you, you'll find the strength to survive each other's bad temper, inhibitions, and habitual exchanges in a constructive manner.

CHANGE OF HEART
Decisive action was necessary when Lucy's attitude to her "open" relationship with Chris began to change (see pages 80–83).

AN OPEN MARRIAGE

Chris had always been open with Lucy about his occasional other women. Now Lucy's business trip to New York was awakening all her insecurities and giving her second thoughts about the "open marriage" agreement they had entered into.

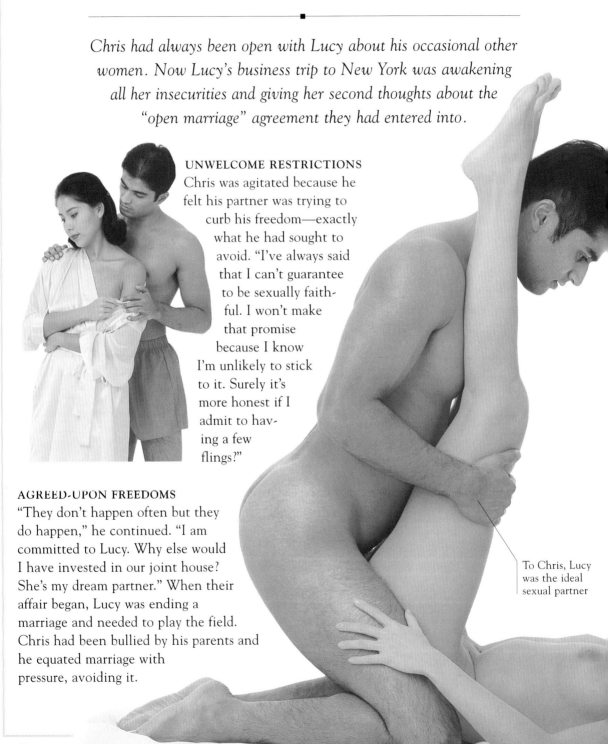

UNWELCOME RESTRICTIONS
Chris was agitated because he felt his partner was trying to curb his freedom—exactly what he had sought to avoid. "I've always said that I can't guarantee to be sexually faithful. I won't make that promise because I know I'm unlikely to stick to it. Surely it's more honest if I admit to having a few flings?"

AGREED-UPON FREEDOMS
"They don't happen often but they do happen," he continued. "I am committed to Lucy. Why else would I have invested in our joint house? She's my dream partner." When their affair began, Lucy was ending a marriage and needed to play the field. Chris had been bullied by his parents and he equated marriage with pressure, avoiding it.

To Chris, Lucy was the ideal sexual partner

SETTLING DOWN

Life on an "open marriage" basis had seemed ideal, and they agreed that, while they could go to bed with other people, each would always consider the other to be the primary partner. Lucy was shaking as she said, "In theory I agree with Chris. I wanted sexual freedoms, too. But I've used them less as I've settled into the relationship. He's been consistent, however, and instead of feeling confident about him, now I'm vulnerable. I feel the minute I leave he'll invite every woman he knows to bed."

CASE NOTES

CHRIS AND LUCY

It was clear that Lucy and Chris had reached a make-or-break point in their relationship, and this was forcing both of them to review it. Lucy was feeling uncertain and vulnerable. She seemed to need a promise of monogamy from Chris, but this was not for him. Instead, both realized that a less emotional approach was needed.

Chris's agreement not to see other women for the time Lucy was away calmed her worries, and when she saw his positive action on her return the relationship stabilized. Best of all, neither partner felt overly compromised in their views or needs.

The "I Should" exercise

Chris and Lucy found the "I Should" exercise (see page 84), listing areas where each felt they "should" change, useful for clarifying their thoughts and concentrating on their promises to each other. It also helped them to visualize what each was offering and being asked to give in order to maintain the relationship.

Lucy was becoming less interested in other men and more settled in her relationship with Chris

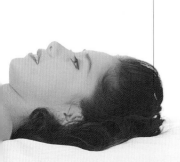

A LOVING WELCOME

Lucy's immediate dilemma was that she was due to go on a business trip and was terribly anxious. "I've got to leave in a couple of weeks," she said. "And I just can't stop crying. I think if Chris can't promise to be more faithful I may have to end things. I can't go on. I want my man to welcome me back with open arms and envelop me with love. But he's quite likely to be in someone else's arms."

Making a Commitment

At first Chris couldn't understand where he was going wrong.
The honesty they established in therapy, however, helped him to
admit his feelings, and between them the couple found areas
for mutually beneficial negotiation.

DEPENDENCE
During counseling, it emerged that Lucy had
left her husband and two children to live with
Chris. She had also gone from being a fairly
wealthy property owner to possessing virtually
nothing. She was now completely
dependent on Chris, not just
emotionally but for her home
and lifestyle and, increasingly, for her sex life.

Lucy translated
her insecurity
into more intense
lovemaking

INSECURITY
As she settled comfortably into her relationship
with Chris, Lucy found that she no longer felt
the desire for other men. But because Chris was
still free to roam, the end result for Lucy was a
sense of great insecurity. In lovemaking she
expressed this with a need for more and
more diversity.

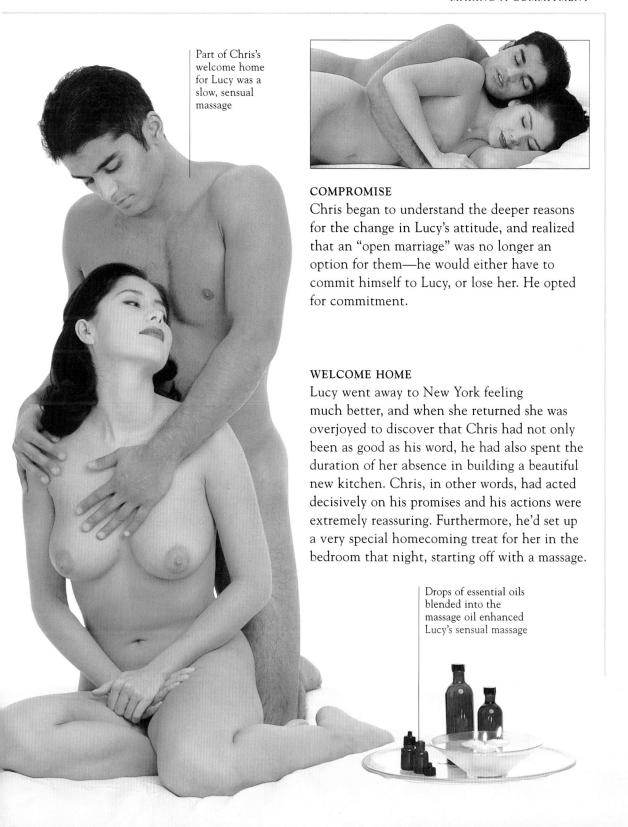

Part of Chris's welcome home for Lucy was a slow, sensual massage

COMPROMISE

Chris began to understand the deeper reasons for the change in Lucy's attitude, and realized that an "open marriage" was no longer an option for them—he would either have to commit himself to Lucy, or lose her. He opted for commitment.

WELCOME HOME

Lucy went away to New York feeling much better, and when she returned she was overjoyed to discover that Chris had not only been as good as his word, he had also spent the duration of her absence in building a beautiful new kitchen. Chris, in other words, had acted decisively on his promises and his actions were extremely reassuring. Furthermore, he'd set up a very special homecoming treat for her in the bedroom that night, starting off with a massage.

Drops of essential oils blended into the massage oil enhanced Lucy's sensual massage

ACTION PLAN

COMMUNICATING WELL *within a relationship means making time for discussion, showing your partner true respect, waiting patiently and listening to any replies that your partner may wish to give, allowing time for him or her to take responsibility for their side of the conversation, and acting on any agreement that arises. There are many simple exercises for improving your communication techniques.*

THE "MAY I?" EXERCISE

This exercise is useful if you tend to say things impulsively, instead of thinking about them first. Instead of simply launching into a conversation or giving your point of view, try to get into the habit of asking "May I?" This will give you time to think before you speak. You should also learn to preface advice with "May I tell you something?" and to accept the answer willingly, whether it is yes or no.

HOLDER OF THE KEYS

If your problem is that one of you constantly interrupts the other, use this technique to overcome it. Only the person holding the keys may speak. When that person is finished, the keys are passed on to the other so that he or she can respond to what has been said. This tactic is borrowed from the Native Americans, whose "talking stick intervention" custom allowed only the person holding the ceremonial stick to speak.

THREE-STAGE COMMUNICATION

If the problem in your relationship is that one of you feels that the other never listens, this exercise will help both of you learn to listen and respond properly when the other initiates a conversation. The basis is that any communication you make must be in three stages:

- *The first speaker makes a statement.*
- *The second speaker replies, making a direct response to what the first speaker has said.*
- *The first speaker must respond to that reply, and what he or she says must in some way relate to it.*

COMPROMISE

The art of breaking an impasse lies in accepting that there has to be a compromise. To make this work:

- *Don't promise the impossible.*
- *Show that you take your partner seriously.*
- *Make a promise about future behavior.*
- *Be sure you can keep the promise.*

HOT AND COLD EXERCISE

This is a very useful way to judge whether you have gone far enough toward meeting the other's needs when negotiating. During your negotiations, stand a few feet apart from each other and place a chair between you. As you talk to each other, each of you must move away from the chair if you feel cold (unsympathetic, angry, distant) toward your partner and nearer the chair if you feel warm or even hot (liking and appreciation).

Since you can actually see how warm your partner is feeling, as demonstrated by his or her moves, you can also understand where you have to make the most effort.

THE "I SHOULD" EXERCISE

This is useful when you and your partner have agreed to make some changes in the pattern of your relationship but are finding it difficult to implement them. You each write a list of the actions you think you ought to take to bring about the changes that you've agreed upon, then number them in terms of difficulty. You then both act on your respective lists, starting with the easiest and working your way up to the most difficult.

(Another useful tactic to employ in this situation is the Yes/No exercise, which is described on page 78).

BODY
LANGUAGE

—————————— • ——————————

*Does your body belie your words? Can you
read true feelings in the way your partner sits
or stands? Learning body language can help
put your partner at ease and will reinforce
your words of love.*

BODY TALK

Body language really is a language. It consists of "sentences" constructed from unconsciously made signals and consciously made gestures. These can be tiny, almost imperceptible movements, or they can involve a shifting of the whole body. If you learn to "speak" in body language, you may find you can use it to steer the feelings and moods of those around you.

When you offer your hand to be shaken, you are using movement deliberately to say "Hello." This is a well-known action that most people recognize as a gesture of goodwill. But if you unconsciously wrap one leg around the other, you may be indicating that you are nervous or tense, while intense finger drumming during a conversation may reinforce angry or impatient words. These last two are less widely recognized acts than a handshake, but are just as telling.

THE BODY SPEAKS

All of us possess unconscious feelings that our body movements betray. The way we move and hold ourselves highlights a whole range of repressed feelings that we may have no desire to communicate by direct speech. This is why an understanding of body language can allow insight into others' true feelings in a situation because you can see what people are "saying" beneath their words.

One of the greatest problems for some people is an inability to reveal and convey how they are feeling. Because many people find it hard to talk about such things, body language is invaluable. Take the case of the "stiff upper lip," for example. When someone looks or sounds stiff it usually means that he or she is in a situation that causes feelings of discomfort or a sense of being "a fish out of water." If you are anxious, you tense yourself in order to take command of the situation or to react to the unknown.

DISPLACEMENT SIGNALS

Tuning into the meaning of what are called "displacement signals" also gives you an advantage. These signals are those apparently meaningless little movements we make such as scratching gently, flicking back the hair, and rubbing the nose. We make these because, without being aware of it, we need to discharge built-up tension. A man with a fidgety leg is telling those around him that he has a lot of energy that he can't use in the present situation, but he's nearly exploding with the need to expend it.

For therapists, an understanding of body language is very useful when talking to clients, because they are often nervous when they first arrive. As the story unfolds, the client may fiddle with his or her hands, lean forward in anguish, or grip the arms of the chair as if for support. If the session goes well and the client feels more in control, he or she may lean back in the chair, hands still, and rearrange his or her arms and legs into a more comfortable and relaxed position. This indicates to the therapist that the session is progressing along positive lines and further progress is possible.

COMMUNICATING THROUGH BODY LANGUAGE

Once you have learned to read and recognize body language you can progress to communication through body and touch. For many people, voicing their fears and worries can be very difficult. If a person bottles up his or her emotions the pressure on that person increases greatly. Often this physical and emotional stress can make itself apparent in minute physical changes that can then be "read" by others.

Strong emotions such as anger, frustration, and confusion often manifest themselves as physical indifference or distance. If a partner feels pressured or taken for granted, he or she may release these emotions through physical coolness toward the other. This in turn may cause the partner to feel that he or she is being punished or that the relationship is over. When this happens it is vital that the true problem be addressed.

A woman, for example, may have used physical coldness in order to chastise her partner for lack of attention. Her partner, feeling that she had simply lost interest in him, may try to win her back by complying with what he sees as her wishes. In other words, he backs off. His attention is further withdrawn and his partner's distress increases. Until she voices her feelings, there may be no way forward for them. Had her part- ner been more aware of the other bodily signs indicating her displeasure, he might have been able to approach her and then caringly draw her fears from her.

BACK IN TOUCH
A gradual reawakening of physical needs through sensual touch quickly brings dividends. Feelings of love that may have been considered to be gone forever are freed to return.

USING BODY LANGUAGE

Next time you watch a successful TV talk-show host in action, watch how he or she avoids looking down or away from the guests or the audience when speaking to them, smiles at every available moment, lifts his or her head to emphasize high spirits, and nods to emphasize a point. What he or she is doing is using body language to communicate warm, positive feelings—such as friendliness and enthusiasm—to the viewers.

Someone with an attractive personality is warm and open, pays attention to whoever he or she is with, and is attentive when listening. He or she will use eye contact to convey attraction and will be flirtatious in a non-pressuring manner. These are all aspects of attractive body language and, if they don't come naturally, they can easily be learned.

Body language reveals many of our more intimate feelings, whether we intend to show them or not.

Another aspect is the ability to interpret the body language of others correctly—it is often easy to misread it—and to respond to it. The listener who ignores hesitations or liveliness is not attractive. One way of conveying your interest is to give small, nonverbal signs, such as nodding at the appropriate times in the conversation, looking directly at the speaker often, and waiting until he or she has looked down and away—the most common sign that someone has finished speaking—before you speak (*see pages 66–67*).

BASIC TECHNIQUES

It is possible to learn how to use body language and how to interpret other people's. There are numerous illustrated books available that describe in detail how to do this, but the basic techniques are quite straightforward. For example, a very effective method of putting people at ease is to "mirror" their body postures.

To do this, you surreptitiously alter the position of your body so that it matches the body posture of the person you are with. This has the effect of making that person relax and feel comfortable. If, after a stint of deliberately emulating your opposite number's movements, you then make some of your own, you'll be interested to see that, if he or she now feels in tune with you, that person will unconsciously copy your movements.

BEING AWARE OF BODY SIGNALS

People you consider attractive often seem attracted to you. When you are sexually interested in a person, you'll probably glance frequently at that person's body, and find your eyes wandering toward the sexual attributes. If that glance is recognized and welcomed, the recipient may move in a way that enhances those sexual parts, "opening" the body and giving you more to look at. If this attention is not welcome, however, the person you are covertly flashing glances at may move in a way that shields his or her more personal parts from your view, or cross arms and legs to create a barrier between the two of you. This would convey the message "you're going too fast for me ," or "I don't want this at the moment" or "I don't want this at all," and you should respond by backing away and letting him or her set the pace.

ANIMAL INSTINCT

Like most animals, a human male goes through the actions of preening as a female approaches. Actions such as straightening the tie, tidying the hair, and brushing specks of dust from the collar and sleeves add up to a show of sexual interest and a desire to attract. A more aggressive display involves hooking the thumbs through the belt. This draws a spectator's eye to the genital region. Although women use preening techniques similar to men's, they have many more methods than men of attracting a partner. The male thumbs-in-belt stance, for example, is carefully modified—one thumb tucked into a belt, handbag, or pants pocket. Women also tend to make more use of their hair, whether it is long or short.

WHAT IS YOUR BODY SAYING?

From childhood we learn to use and respond to body language. Few people do not recognize, even unconsciously, the stance of anger or a look of fear, yet there are aspects of your own body language that you may not notice, but that your partner undoubtedly will.

When you are attracted to someone it can be for many reasons. Perhaps he or she is delicate and shy, bringing out the mothering or "knight in shining armor" response in you. On the other hand, it may be strength of character and self-assurance, shown in an upright posture and confident gaze, that you find attractive.

Whatever the reasons, the initial attraction will be bound up in what your partner's body language says, and if this message changes over time, your feelings may well change, too. If this happens, and either of you is unhappy with the change, it is vital that both of you learn and understand exactly what messages are being conveyed.

FLIRTING

Possibly one of the best and most widely known uses of body language is flirting. The range of courtship gestures, from the subtle to the blatant, have been examined, noted and practiced for centuries. It can be fascinating to watch men and women mixing socially and trying to spot the more obvious aspects of flirtation in their body language.

MISSING MESSAGES

Bob and Nikki (see pages 90–93) nearly lost the respect and intimacy in their relationship because of Bob's body language.

A MATURING RELATIONSHIP

People who have lived together for a while may abandon their best behavior and reveal the real personalities lurking underneath. Bob and Nikki's relationship faltered because his "real" personality was childish, and Nikki didn't find it sexy.

EARLY EXPECTATIONS

Most people want to remain in love but don't expect the romance to live forever. The accepted pattern of a good relationship seems to be that the state of being "in love" lasts for the first couple of years, but it then turns into something less intense but much more tender. If we're lucky it is this deep affection that lets lovemaking continue. Bob thought his younger second wife, Nikki, the sexiest thing on legs when they first met. "She could do pretty well what she liked with me," he joked.

Nikki felt her desire for Bob diminishing

GROWING APART

Bob found it hard to grasp that this early stage of the relationship had ended. He seriously thought something was wrong. "In the last few years, especially since the birth of our second child, Nikki just seems to have lost interest," he complained. "Do all women get bored with sex eventually?" he asked. "Or is it simply that there's something wrong with Nikki?"

Many men find a woman who knows how to take control very exciting, and Bob was no exception

BODY TALK

Nikki had a rather different perspective. "The trouble is I've learned to think of Bob as one of the children, despite the fact that he's older than me.

Not a lot is different in bed. He lies on the bed with all his clothes on, expecting me to undress him and get him going sexually. There's really not much in it for me."

MAN OR BOY?

Nikki admitted that in the early days she had enjoyed being the sexual innovator, and her version of events provided an insight into why she was losing interest in sex. When an adult behaves like a child, it's very hard to see him or her as an erotic object. And Nikki, being an honest, extrovert woman, couldn't pretend to desire someone who behaved more like a baby in bed than a lover, even though she missed the intimacy terribly.

Nikki desperately wanted to regain the passion and intimacy she and Bob had enjoyed

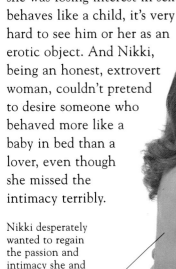

CASE NOTES

BOB AND NIKKI

It is not uncommon for a couple's sexual relationship to change when they become parents. Sometimes, the woman feels that the uninhibited sexuality that she enjoyed previously is incompatible with the responsibilities of motherhood (see page 22). In other cases, some men find they are less attracted to their partners after the birth, while others, like Bob, unwittingly adopt a childlike role and expect to be "mothered."

Whatever the change in attitude of either partner, the other is often able to adapt and it does not become a problem. But to Nikki, Bob's unintended but tediously childlike behavior was a sexual turn-off, and it was his behavior and body language, rather than anything he said or consciously intended, that conveyed his attitude to his partner.

The power of touch

Resolving Bob and Nikki's problem was relatively simple once Bob had grasped the signals his body language was giving (see page 106). He understood the problem and accepted his responsibility for it. The next step was for him to rebuild his emotional relationship with Nikki and then reestablish their physical relationship. Sensual massage was useful as it let him take an active and unselfish role.

Getting Back in Touch

*During the counseling sessions, Bob gradually realized that he
had changed his view of Nikki after she became a parent, with
the result that he treated her like a mother, too. Once he had
accepted this he was spurred to change his approach to her.*

Nikki had to express her
frustration to her husband

FOND MEMORIES

One of the key stages in Bob's acceptance of
his responsibility for the problem came when
Nikki compared the way he used to be with his
current behavior. In those early days he had
listened to her, joined in with her enthusiasms,
and been a caring and sensitive lover. How
could he have changed so much?

Heated arguments between them revealed the
answer, especially when Nikki brought up the
striking imagery of Bob lying on his back on
the bed, waiting for her to undress him—
from such body language, it
sounded as if Bob had
reverted to babyhood.

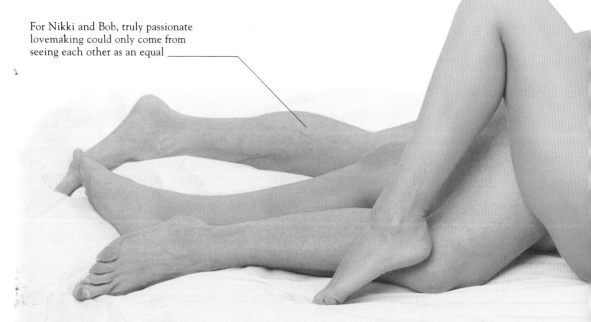

For Nikki and Bob, truly passionate
lovemaking could only come from
seeing each other as an equal

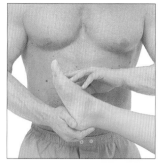

ACCEPTANCE

The couple decided that, through seeing Nikki with their children, Bob had started taking her for granted, as if she were also his parent. When Bob grasped this picture of himself as an overgrown child rather than an older and responsible husband, he was very upset. Fortunately, he needed little instruction on becoming a more mature lover, but to give themselves the best possible chance the couple practiced sensual massage (*see page 106*) at home.

MAKING THE CHANGE

When the couple finished their therapy, Bob decided to quit his job so that he could help his wife expand her growing gardening business. Sexually, he made a point of pleasuring his wife at least as often as she approached him.

When Bob realized what he had been missing by seeing Nikki as a mother figure, they soon regained the spark in their lovemaking

BODY LANGUAGE IN BED

Sex can spell out what sort of mood your partner is in at the time and how relaxed or anxious he or she is feeling. It can also tell you how good you are at tuning in to your partner's moods and interpreting his or her body language. It can be very interesting to learn to read and respond to the body language of sex.

Let's begin at the beginning of a loving encounter—those moves leading up to sex. You've been kissing like crazy on the sofa or even rolling around on the floor. "Let's go to bed," one of you says. "Yes," breathes the other. On wings of pure arousal, you fly together into the bedroom. But you don't just tear off each other's clothes. Suddenly the practicalities of undressing and going to bed get in the way and slow you down. During this temporary interruption to your lovemaking, you will be able to learn a lot about your partner's feelings from his or her behavior and body language—for example, whether he or she is nervous or inhibited. And you can learn a lot about your partner's character from his or her overall behavior.

NERVOUSNESS

Your partner is sitting up in bed waiting for you. She has taken her clothes off and is hunched forward, staring straight down at the bedclothes and clasping her hands tightly around her knees. This pose should tell you that your partner is feeling tense; she may be wondering if she is doing the right thing. The best solution is for you to get into bed beside her and hold out your arms for a huge cuddle. That will reassure her that you want her for herself and that you care that she feels comfortable. It won't be long before the cuddling works its magic and she relaxes into a passionate embrace.

Bedroom body language can tell you just how your partner is feeling without a word being spoken.

Another possibility is that your partner hasn't followed through the romantic and sexy preliminaries but instead is rushing in and out of the bathroom, hanging his clothes neatly over a chair, and brushing his teeth. It all seems to take an eternity, and when he finally comes to bed he directs his attention all around the room, focusing on anything, it seems, except you. All this may add up to the fact that he, too, is nervous. If this is the case, take him in your arms and cuddle him until he calms down.

STIFFNESS

But what if your partner has readily got into bed with you but is lying very stiffly next to you without touching you? The fact that you shared such closeness moments earlier makes it unlikely that your partner has lost enthusiasm, so you may assume that he is uncomfortable and is tensing himself to take charge of the situation. Maybe he is the type of man who feels that all the responsibility is his and that he must appear to be in control at all costs. A solution to his tenseness would be a massage (*see page 101*), so offer him one immediately and ask him not to move a muscle for the next ten minutes. (He might find this request difficult to comply with while you are massaging him!)

INHIBITIONS

On getting into bed, your partner turns her back on you and draws her knees up, curling into a fetal position. This fairly clearly shows that she has become filled with inhibitions and may be wondering how she can go through with sex.

The best remedy for such fears is an encompassing cuddle, spoons-style. Hold her in your arms and alter your breathing until it matches hers. Then, slowly but surely, start to make each breath longer and more relaxed. With any luck, your partner will copy and begin to relax. If not, massage will help, but don't rush your partner into sex from a comfortable massage if he or she is not ready.

CHARACTER ANALYSIS

The way a person acts before, during, and after lovemaking has always seemed to offer a unique and fairly reliable method of predicting just what sort of partner that person will be and what he or she will bring to the relationship as a whole. This is not a foolproof system of analysis, but it can alert you to certain personality traits that you may or may not find compatible with your own.

The person who is greedy for intercourse and can't be bothered to spend much time on foreplay is likely to be impatient and possibly spoiled. This person may simply be very needy for sex, however, and may well improve with time.

The person who goes straight for intercourse, with no attempt at foreplay, then finishes rapidly and doesn't bother with his or her partner's satisfaction, is downright selfish. But the person who loves playing before intercourse, with a lot of rolling around and fun and games, is usually childlike in the best sense of the word and is going to be easy and fun to have a relationship with.

READING ACTIONS
Tom quickly realized that there was a problem with his relationship with Lynn (see pages 96–99) when he found her body language disconcerting and unattractive.

SERIOUS COMPETITION

*These days, most people accept that masturbation is simply
a normal part of life. But Tom felt hurt and threatened when his
partner, Lynn, began to get more pleasure from masturbation
than from making love.*

SEEKING HELP

Tom sought counseling on his own. He thought that Lynn's
liking for masturbation indicated that she had a problem
with sex, and he wanted to work out the best ways in which
he might deal with her. He appeared to be a well-adjusted
young man, without sexual hangups and with few
difficulties in talking about sex. Yet inhibitions
were partly the subject of his concern. He'd been
made to feel inhibited by his girlfriend and now he
was feeling confused.

New romance is
often highly spiced
and passionate

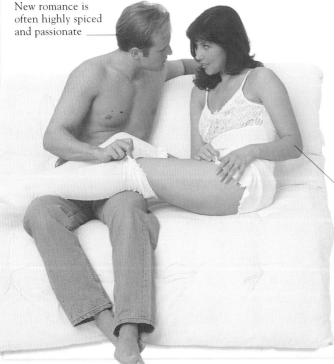

EARLY PASSION

Tom explained that he had had several
girlfriends and lived with the last for three
years. "I've been in a new relationship,
with Lynn, for three months. We fell for
each other dramatically and she moved
into my apartment a month ago. I thought
we'd never be out of bed."

Finding the perfect
partner can seem to
come out of the blue

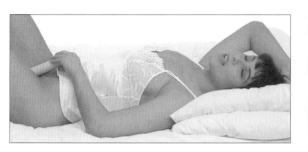

SEX GAMES?

"But something very odd is going on," he said. "To begin with, I thought she was just teasing me, but now I'm really uncomfortable about it all. Every night, she disappears into the bedroom before me, and when I eventually follow she's lying on the bed, masturbating with her vibrator. She's playing some sort of game and it's a real turn-off."

Sex aids can be great, but only if both partners enjoy them

CASE NOTES

●

TOM AND LYNN

Tom's concern about Lynn's behavior was made worse because he could not understand the reason for it. He was also worried by Lynn's implied suggestion that he had an inhibition problem, and that suggestion was what had prompted him to seek counseling.

Warning signs

As it turned out, the problem was Lynn's, but instead of talking it through with Tom she had expressed it through her body language and behavior. Had Tom spotted the subtle clues contained in Lynn's behavior and body language, especially in bed (see page 106), he could have acted sooner and lessened the emotional toll that the experience had taken on him.

SPOILED CHILD

"I've asked her what it's all about, but she sort of brushes me off, implying that I've got an inhibition problem," Tom continued. "She then claims that if I really loved her, I wouldn't mind that she wants to give herself a good time. That's all very well, but if this is going to be every night, what am I supposed to think? Am I inhibited? She's like a spoiled child with a toy."

Taking Charge

•

It sounded as if Lynn was just as interested in the attention that her masturbation provoked as she was in sexual self-satisfaction. Fortunately, through therapy, Tom realized that if he was to save his relationship he had to discover why this was.

FACING THE FACTS

Tom didn't want to slant the story so that Lynn would appear as as the "bad guy." But, by telling his story in detail, Tom became convinced that there was something abnormal about the situation and her behavior. When asked to consider what he thought it was all about, he replied, "It seems deliberate. If she masturbated only occasionally, that would be fine. But every night?"

The importance of the vibrator drove a wedge between the couple

FALSE MOVES

After the first counseling session, Tom felt strong enough to confront Lynn. Her response was to offer oral sex. It felt good at the time, Tom admitted, but that evening, Lynn was back in the bedroom with the vibrator.

Lynn shied away from the real problem, covering it with a show of passion

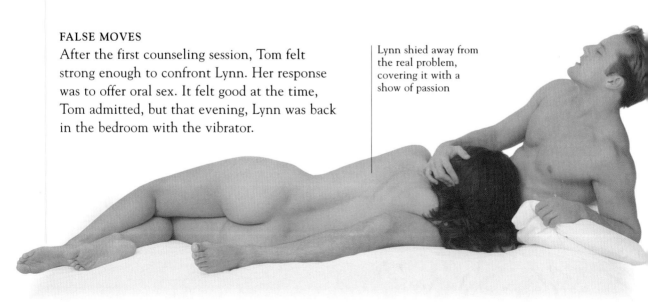

COMFORT AND TRUST

As soon as Tom realized this, his reaction was to hold Lynn close. He promised that he wouldn't let her down and that she didn't need to distance herself from him with the vibrator. Lynn clung to him and shuddered as she relaxed. That night the couple celebrated their love passionately.

REALIZATION

Then he got mad and used his anger for a confrontation. She told him that the vibrator did not let her down like men did and that he was selfish for even questioning her. This triggered a memory in Tom from the counseling session. At the time he hadn't been sure, but now his answer to the question "Is Lynn insecure?" was "Yes."

Tom showed his true feelings for Lynn with passion and tenderness

Able to relax, Lynn gave herself to Tom and proved her trust in him

USING TOUCH

Touch is a vital part of a loving relationship. It is a reassurance, a healer, a pleasure, and a language. For instance, a warm caress means "I love you," and a friendly hug says, "I like you and I'm pleased to see you."

If we are lucky, we and our partners will use touch spontaneously and creatively. Almost instinctively, we will stroke a lover's arm, kiss on many parts of the body, and walk holding hands or with arms wrapped around each other. We may do this without thinking, because we were brought up by parents who we saw hug each other and show their mutual affection in countless physical ways, which set an example for us. Not all of us were so lucky, however, and sadly, men and women with cold parents often have to learn to use touch because they did not learn it in childhood.

IMPROVING BEDTIME TOUCH

If you haven't learned to be sensual, you may want help in improving your lovemaking techniques. Although sex is not the only criterion on which a relationship is made or broken, it is generally agreed that when sex (for which you can also read sensuality) doesn't work well, the relationship often erodes from within. If you dread doing something premeditated, you won't want to surprise your lover by announcing that you are going to give him or her a massage instead of having intercourse. But you might like to change your bedtime routine just slightly. For example, try lying side by side and touching your partner all over. If he or she feels like responding, that's wonderful. If you are not in the habit of cuddling, try moving into the spoons position. Snuggle into your partner's back with your arms around his or her waist, and synchronize your breathing.

Recharging a relationship using physical contact, particularly intimate touch, can be great fun and very rewarding.

OFFER A MASSAGE

If you can face up to making a deliberate change in your bedtime routine, substitute an erotic massage for intercourse. For both of you to enjoy this fully, you need to be in agreement beforehand that you will take turns. If only one partner receives sensual pleasure while the other always gives it, eroticism becomes unbalanced and the giver ends up resentful.

It is no accident that massage is used as the basis for much sex therapy. It can actually teach you how to communicate in bed. It concentrates stimulation on the areas that feel wonderful when touched, so that physical sensations are enhanced, and it makes you feel so much warmer toward each other that you become nicer people to live with.

Preparing for Massage

Make sure that the room in which you are going to give the massage is warm and draft-free, and that you are not going to be disturbed (don't hesitate to lock the door if necessary). To be effective, a massage should be given with the recipient lying on a firm surface, and most beds are too soft for this. So spread warmed towels on the floor to create a comfortable massaging surface, and have your bottle of massage oil—also warmed, by standing it in a small bowl of warm water—within easy reach and also on a bed of towels in case of spillage. Make sure that your fingernails are not broken or rough-edged, wash your hands thoroughly in hot water, and ensure that they are warm when you begin giving the massage.

Massage Strokes

The three basic strokes to use when giving a massage are circling, swimming, and kneading. Because circling is such a good basic stroke it can be used on almost any part of the body, but is especially effective on the fleshier areas. Circling consists of placing the palms of both hands on the body and moving them in circles, outward and away from the spine.

Swimming strokes can be given up and down all the fleshy parts of the body, including the buttocks. Move your hands, palms down, in circles but in opposite directions, taking on a kind of swimming sensation. It's a good idea to include the buttocks as often as possible because they are among the most sensual parts of the body. Kneading is carried out by visualizing your partner's flesh as soft dough. Take pinches of it between fingers and thumb, rhythmically squeezing and releasing it. When you are practiced at kneading, you'll be able to squeeze the flesh so that it travels from one hand to the other in a wavelike motion. The more fleshy the area to be massaged, the deeper the kneading action can be.

The secret to making such a massage really sensual is to vary the pressure you exert. Start each stroke using firm pressure, and each time you repeat it, reduce the pressure until you are massaging with the lightest of fingertip touch. Last of all, caress your partner all over with your fingernails, moving them in a variety of ways to maximize the sensual effect. Start off moving them in circles, then change to up-and-down and side-to-side movements, varying the lengths of the strokes.

WARMTH MOVES
If you have difficulty learning how to express your feelings physically, try the following moves:
• Look into each other's eyes longer than usual
• Stand or sit closer together than normal
• Smile at each other more than usual
• Make gentle, affectionate physical contact, such as holding hands or putting your arms around each other.

LEARNING TO TOUCH
Andrew and Vicki (see pages 102–105) saved their relationship and reaffirmed their feelings through touch.

DRIFTING APART

●

*When lovers report that they are growing apart, they sometimes
mean literally as well as emotionally. Andrew and Vicki led
very busy lives and regretted that this had forced them apart to
such an extent that lovemaking had virtually ceased.*

STOLEN MOMENTS

If you were brought up by parents who spent
every possible moment together, it comes as a
shock to wake up one day and realize that you
and your loved one haven't
actually met in the same
house for over three
weeks. Yet such is
the shape of work
these days that we
often have to take
jobs wherever we
can get them. If the
job involves a lot of
traveling, as Vicki's
did, it may mean
that you spend much
less time at home
than you would
like to. "But at
least it made the
homecomings
sexy," said Vicki.
"Time was when I'd
walk into the house and
find Andrew waiting for
me in bed."

PRESSURES OF WORK

Absences can be divisive if there are too many
for too long. Vicki appeared subdued when she
explained, "I set up exhibitions and shows
around the country, so I'm always on the road.
It's tough readjusting when I'm home. Usually,
it's time to leave again just when our sex life
has improved. I leave Andrew thinking about
lovemaking, and have to turn myself off again."

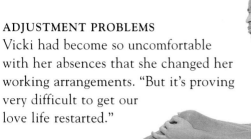

ADJUSTMENT PROBLEMS

Vicki had become so uncomfortable with her absences that she changed her working arrangements. "But it's proving very difficult to get our love life restarted."

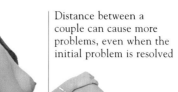

Distance between a couple can cause more problems, even when the initial problem is resolved

UNCERTAINTY

Andrew told a slightly different story. "Vicki and I had a very good sex life when we first dated, but it dwindled once Vicki moved in. I think that's because I was taken by surprise when she arrived. I'd never lived with anyone before and I wasn't sure I wanted her there. But while we've been talking, I've realized that I love her very much and I want to make it work."

Loving intimacy between a couple can outweigh many problems

Reawakening Desire

Andrew's confession that he'd felt invaded by Vicki settling into his home, then angry about her comings and goings, had helped him realize that what he wanted from the relationship was to make things work with her.

PASSIVE RESISTANCE

Accepting the diminished sex and doing nothing to improve things was Andrew's way of following a pattern of passive resistance that he had learned in childhood. He acknowledged this and realized he did not want to feel like this about Vicki. "I'd really like to make love to you again," he told her directly. Vicki became very tearful when she heard him say this and realized his true feelings for her.

Run long hair along your lover's chest and stomach

Gently caress your partner's body with your fingertips

Give up your body completely to your partner and relax

MUTUAL PLEASURING

They both realized that resuming lovemaking might be difficult, and agreed to start by using a sensual touch routine without intercourse. This routine consisted of erotic massage and mutual masturbation, and it helped them reestablish the physical side of their relationship.

Intimate massage should lead to a natural return to lovemaking

CASE NOTES

ANDREW AND VICKI

When her sex life with Andrew all but disappeared, Vicki thought that the reason was her frequent absences from home. So she was surprised to find that spending more time at home brought no improvement, and then gladdened when, during counseling, she learned a new approach.

It can be difficult to reestablish the physical side of a relationship once it's faded. Erotic massage (see pages 101 and 106) and mutual masturbation gave Andrew and Vicki time to rediscover each other without the pressures of intercourse.

RETURN TO HAPPINESS

At a follow-up session six weeks later, Andrew and Vicki smilingly agreed that the sensual touch routine had been a great success. They had resumed intercourse within a week.

ACTION PLAN

IF YOU LEARN TO read your partner's body language, you will be able to pick up on any subtle signs that indicate he or she is not happy about something. You'll also become aware of what your body language says to others, and learn to ensure that it is conveying the right impression. And remember, the most direct form of body language—touch—is a great way to communicate loving feelings to your partner.

BEDROOM BODY LANGUAGE

How physically close you get to your partner often indicates how intimate you are feeling. This may seem obvious, but signals given off through body language can reveal a great deal about a person's, or a couple's, feelings.

When people feel very in tune with each other, they can often be seen in matching poses, in which their bodily postures are mirroring each other.

Learning to read body language is particularly useful in the bedroom, when actions are used to express possibly embarrassing intentions and desires.

Look out for the telltale signs of a person who is unlikely to be looking for sexual intimacy. His or her legs or arms may be drawn close to the body, eye contact may be limited, and there even may be an actual "barrier," for example, a book held up to the face, or a tightly wrapped bathrobe. Coy behavior can also be a means of maintaining a discouraging distance between a person and his or her prospective lover.

Examples of encouraging and discouraging body language might be:

- *If your partner is lying in bed, smiling, with his or her arms wide open, the chances are you're being offered a cuddle.*
- *If your partner is sitting on the edge of the bed, looking down with a slight frown, cheek resting in hand, and arms pressed close to the body, you could surmise that he or she is nervous about making love.*

These are not necessarily the only answers, but they are likely ones. Your ability to interpret them depends not just on obvious body language but also your knowledge of your partner; it may be that your partner thinks you'll be aroused by the indifference shown by studiously reading in bed. Learn as much as you can about your partner, in case something is going on that you haven't recognized.

EROTIC MASSAGE

Using the three basic strokes, circling, swimming, and kneading (*see page 101*), offer your partner a simple massage. Once comfortable with massage and confident about touching each other, you may like to incorporate some erotic ideas:

- *Give your partner a head massage.*
- *Slowly, with one fingertip, circle the inside of the ear, tracing its outline.*
- *Breathe softly into the ear.*
- *Breathe onto the neck.*
- *Draw your fingernails down the inner arm.*
- *Circle the nipples and areolae with your fingernail.*
- *Softly pinch the nipples between finger and thumb.*
- *Stroke the sides of the breasts.*
- *Breathe on the nipples.*
- *If you have long hair, sweep it across your partner's abdomen.*
- *Circle the abdomen with your fingertips.*
- *Run your fingertips up the inner thigh, stopping at the genitals.*
- *Repeat but finish by brushing against the genitals.*
- *Deep massage your partner's palm.*
- *Circle the palms with your fingertips.*
- *Gently and slowly pull a finger between each of the toes.*

Concentrate on any move that your partner particularly likes, and stop immediately if he or she asks you to or shows any discomfort.

ENHANCING INTIMACY

Trust and honesty can make or break an intimate relationship. Unless both are maintained you may need help to reestablish an environment in which they, and ultimately your relationship, can thrive.

SOCIAL AND SEXUAL FACTORS

Many people make the mistake of thinking that intimacy is only about sex. By now, this book should have made it clear that intimacy is about the whole state of your relationship and not just one aspect. It should also have become apparent that if you feel upset in nonsexual sides of your relationship, the problem may well affect what goes on in bed.

This chapter looks at how sexual intimacy between two people can change over time or because of external influences such as work, and how sexual myth and ignorance are capable of obstructing your love life. One invaluable theory that the Institute for the Advanced Study of Human Sexuality, in San Francisco, has codified is that called a socio-response cycle. According to the theory, this socio-response cycle functions in parallel with the sexual response cycle *(see page 116)* and roughly simultaneously with it: in order to make love, you also have to relate to people. The socio-response cycle consists of four major components, these being vague unrest, options, negotiations, and expectations. This sounds very complicated but is actually quite straightforward.

VAGUE UNREST
During this phase of the socio-response cycle, a man or woman becomes aware of his or her possibilities and options. He or she needs other people (partners) and has to relate to them. In order to do this, he or she must go on to examine the available options.

OPTIONS
Everyone has options—that is, the choices they are allowed to make and the choices they allow themselves to make. This is as true of sexual lifestyles as it is of social ones, and you can learn to expand your options and improve your sexual life. For example, one sexual option is to understand that you can make love to your partner with many different areas of your body instead of confining your lovemaking solely to your genitals.

These options are available to everyone, and not everyone will choose to accept or focus on the same ones. The choice of options is one that must be agreed by each individual couple, and there are no fixed rules.

NEGOTIATIONS

Once you've examined the options and decided to go into action, you move on to negotiations. The resulting agreement that you make, either consciously or unconsciously, with a partner, is what decides the quality of the sex you'll get. And, of course, the negotiations are affected by your partner's options as well as your own, and you must be prepared to review your chosen options if they are in conflict with your partner's.

THE IMPORTANCE OF NEGOTIATION

Within relationships, negotiation is important because it can be the means of getting out of paralyzing sex roles. As a strategy for making a boring sexual activity tolerable, lying back and thinking of England is not only unsatisfactory, it is also an unskilled negotiation, one that you haven't thought through fully in any way.

A premature ejaculator, for example, might be a bad negotiator, and so might his partner. In some cases, men who suffer from premature ejaculation are men who think of sex as something to be carried out rapidly, and even furtively. There's not much emphasis on negotiation with the female partner here, which is doubly sad since premature ejaculation is one of the easiest sex problems to overcome. Unusual sex needs are often non-negotiable. A voyeur or an obscene phone caller violates another person's space. Therefore, in this situation, any negotiation stops before it's begun. You cannot "agree" with force and coercion.

EXPECTATIONS

Unrealistic expectations on either side can influence the entire quality of a relationship (see pages 20–25). It is unreasonable, for example, to expect someone's goals to change just because yours have. A woman who loses interest in sex because her partner refuses to get her pregnant (when they had long ago agreed not to have children) is being unreasonable to herself, and unfair to her partner, too. He's only going along with the agreement that they originally made.

SEXUAL INTIMACY
When a couple achieves a strong, comfortable intimacy with each other, many aspects of the relationship, including the quality of their communication and lovemaking, will benefit from it.

SEARCH FOR INTIMACY

Sexual intimacy is that inner sense of loving and being loved that nestles at the very core of a relationship. Although there are several ways of experiencing that sense of intimacy, the route via sex is a marvelous one. If that intimacy is lost within a relationship, then we lose something integral, for it is said that you can often judge the state of play in other areas of a marriage from how well the two partners cooperate in bed.

Our attitudes about sex, as we have seen, are built up for each individual from childhood. Family opinions, learned morals, and experience all contribute to how successfully we offer and accept intimacy. It is this intimacy, for example, that will drive a man, on realizing he is impotent, to continue to demonstrate his love for his wife with kissing and caresses. This shows that their relationship is strong enough to weather difficult times.

If, on the other hand, he uses his impotence as an excuse for not touching his wife sexually again, it is fair to assume that the love between them has waned and that there is little intimacy left. Often couples who have strong and loving relationships, good marriages with good sex lives, are searching for something different, only they're not sure exactly what they want. The phantom of faint dissatisfaction is insidious. Before you know it you may be risking your perfectly good marriage over a half-hearted affair. It's certainly a moment of truth, but one that is usually passed up for fear of admitting the worst—the end of a relationship.

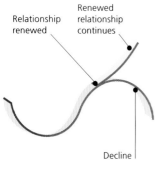

Renewed relationship continues

Relationship renewed

Decline

Curve of relationship if not renewed

Curve of renewed relationship

THE SIGMOID CURVE
Any relationship can be seen in terms of growth periods, peaks, and periods of decline. Drawn as a graph, the series of ups and downs of any relationship traces a distinct S-shape, or sigmoid curve. If the relationship is renewed before the curve goes into decline, a new upward curve begins.

UPS AND DOWNS

Charles Handy, a business educationalist, has identified a point in business relationships where all parties should begin preparing for something new, even though the present activity is still successful. The reason for this is that any relationship can be seen in terms of growth periods, peaks, and periods of decline. Drawn as a graph, the series of ups and downs of any relationship traces a distinct S-shape, or sigmoid curve.

This may sound depressing if it means that all relationships will eventually go into a decline but, as Handy says, "Luckily there is life beyond the curve. The secret of constant growth is to start a new sigmoid curve before the first one peters out" and to make sure that it starts in the right place—just before the first curve reaches its peak. Handy goes on to say that every relationship will need a second curve. Too often couples hang on to their old habits, but he also admits that the transition can be difficult, especially if you try to preserve the best of the old curve and instil the common sense of the new.

APPLYING THE SIGMOID CURVE

Although Handy offers no practical applications of the curve, the emotional approach needed to view your relationship in these terms can be illustrated through two examples from group therapy. One woman, married for seven years, wanted to move to a new house. Her husband refused, believing their house perfectly adequate. What he didn't realize was that his wife was voicing a need for change, and not just of a home. Their relationship curve continued downward and the marriage failed. Another woman, however, in the same situation, was asked by her husband to look inside herself. He had sensed that her restlessness had nothing to do with where they lived. She considered this and agreed that he was right. Her soul-searching initiated the second upward curve of their relationship.

For the second couple, the second curve brought them closer together as both felt they were being honest and trusting with each other. Both had to work hard toward a more fulfilling life, but with each other's support they were able to feel better about their future together and happier in their family life. They also felt their sexual encounters had been enriched. Their closeness was rejuvenated. Focusing on the true problem instead of a convenient substitute enabled them to grow closer, just as it did for Aline and Robert (see pages 112–115).

SEX AND INTIMACY

One way of dealing with the sexual itch is to recognize that there is something wrong with your relationship, even if you can't see what it is. No matter how familiar the two of you are, perhaps your sense of intimacy is slipping. To get it back you may need to voice those long-silent yet heartfelt words of love, reveal any doubts you may have, and generally open up about your feelings, however painful this may be.

When you are able to do this, and realize that your partner loves you despite your fears, that special inner core feels renewed. Of course, this may seem like a terribly risky thing to do, as it may well be. Yet it is unlikely that you will feel that special feeling without taking the risk and trusting your partner. The difficulty is in recognizing when to re-examine your love and your sex life. Waiting until restlessness sets in may be too late, but why begin to change the dynamic of the relationship if you are both perfectly happy with it?

RENEWING INTIMACY
Aline and Robert (see pages 112–115) saved their relationship when they realized, and acted on, the true causes of their problems.

TOO TIRED FOR SEX

When a partner moves into the spare room, even if it's for an innocent reason, one of the sad side-effects is that feelings of intimacy slip away. Aline was becoming increasingly distressed by what felt like the loss of her partner, Robert.

POOR SLEEP

There are times when problems of intimacy, even though they give the impression of being emotionally caused, are due to physical changes. Sleep difficulties can be the result of tension between partners, but they can also be a side effect of the menopause or something as unromantic as digestive problems.

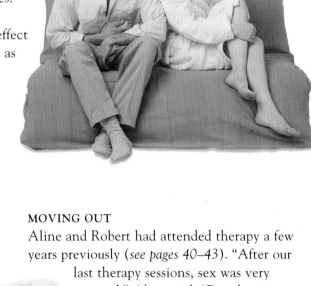

Physical problems and disturbed sleep can trouble a relationship

MOVING OUT

Aline and Robert had attended therapy a few years previously (*see pages 40–43*). "After our last therapy sessions, sex was very good," Aline said. "But about a year ago, both of us started to have sleep problems. Robert became impossible to share a bed with because he heaved and turned half the night, getting up frequently and stomping around. In desperation I began sleeping in the spare room. We still made love quite often, but gradually it stopped."

DRIFTING APART

"Sleeping alone helped both of us at first," said Aline, "but when sex dwindled, I didn't know if it was my fault or Robert's. To make matters worse I began to sleep badly myself. I always feel tired now, never feel like sex, and find it much harder to have climaxes. I feel very warm toward Robert after lovemaking but that warmth disappears. He's even stopped letting me share the bathroom with him because suddenly he's embarrassed to have me see his body. I miss the intimacy with him desperately."

FOND MEMORIES

Robert was embarrassed by his wife's words. "Of course sex isn't happening as often as it used to be, but that's probably just because we're getting older. I won't say I wouldn't want to improve things. But my stomach problems are making that impossible."

Warm memories of their good times together gave Aline and Robert the incentive to take action

Restoring Desire

Aline and Robert investigated the possible reasons for their sleeplessness and, by ensuring that they received medical attention for their sleep problems, soon regained the love and intimacy that had been missing from their sex life.

MEDICAL PROBLEMS

Neither Aline nor Robert had consulted a doctor about their sleep difficulties, nor had Robert consulted anyone about his chronic indigestion. It hadn't occurred to him it could be anything other than aging. And although Aline was clearly a middle-aged woman going into menopause, because she was only 43 it hadn't occurred to her that this could be the cause of her problem. Tests also revealed that Robert had a duodenal ulcer.

Aline soon felt revived and refreshed with desires she thought had long since gone ——————

EFFECTIVE TREATMENT

The special diet and medication Robert was prescribed helped him sleep better. He also started exercising regularly to get into shape. Blood tests showed that Aline's levels of the hormone estrogen were low, and the doctor prescribed a replacement dose. Within three months she felt like a new woman, and her first decision, following their return to counseling, was to move back into the marital bedroom.

INTIMATE MASSAGE

This couple didn't really need much more help. But because they had both experienced a loss of sexual confidence, mutual self-pleasuring, in the form of erotic massage (*see pages 101 and 106*), would benefit them. Massage gave them a means of getting back in touch with each other on an intimate physical level without feeling self-conscious about doing so. Three months later, their sense of sexual intimacy was restored and, in addition, each felt physically fit and well for the first time in years.

CASE NOTES

■

ALINE AND ROBERT

Many people, when they reach middle age, think that any changes in their health, fitness, or sexual appetite are due simply to the process of aging and assume that nothing can be done about them. This is a mistake because, as Aline and Robert found, many such changes are easily cured—it makes no sense to ignore them and let them blight your life. (Ignoring them can lead to potentially serious illnesses being left undiagnosed and therefore untreated.)

Fortunately, Aline and Robert found effective remedies for their medical problems. Once those had been dealt with, rebuilding their sex life with the help of massage (see pages 101 and 106) *and the Small Moves Exercise* (see page 122) *was simple and straightforward.*

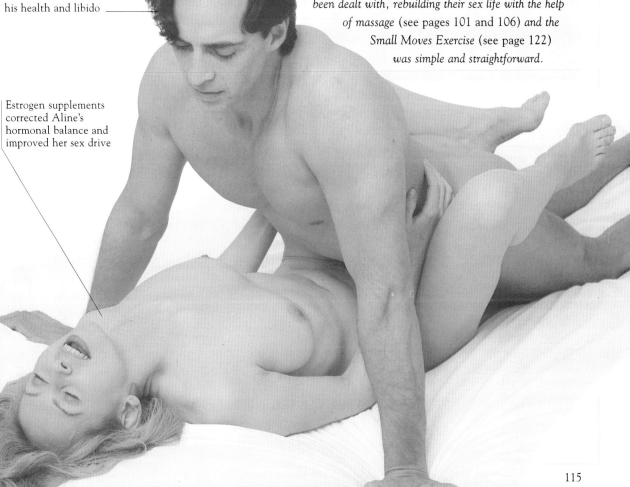

Medication, diet, and exercise cured Robert's insomnia and restored his health and libido

Estrogen supplements corrected Aline's hormonal balance and improved her sex drive

INCREASING INTIMACY

As we grow older we build up a store of misunderstandings and myths about sex and sexuality that can be universal in their existence or unique to ourselves. But whatever their foundation, misconceptions about sex can cause problems between couples when each believes the other to be reacting to them personally, rather than through the blinkered and unrealistic views they've developed about sexual intercourse.

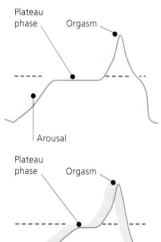

Plateau phase — Orgasm

Arousal

Plateau phase — Orgasm

Arousal

___/ MALE ___/ FEMALE

SEXUAL RESPONSE
Men and women have very different responses to sexual stimulation. Men need a relatively short period of arousal that tends to be followed by a relatively long plateau phase. Women in general need a longer period of stimulation, followed by a shorter plateau phase, before reaching orgasm.

Many men and women suffer from false ideas about sex. One very common belief is that all women have the same sexual response, and that all will climax in the same way if certain formulaic foreplay is carried out. Other myths include the idea that women need the same type of sexual stimulation as men or that masturbation can make you blind, deaf, or insane, or even kill you. The truth is that masturbation, in private, has been found to relieve physical tension and provide a sensual and enjoyable experience.

DISPELING MYTHS

In many situations where one partner has false ideas about sex, many difficulties can be avoided if the other partner feels confident enough to voice his or her uncertainty or dissatisfaction. Unfortunately, it can be easier to think of yourself as being wrong than to question these myths.

Sexual myths, such as the idea that masturbation can lead to blindness, often become the basis for jokes. But if you are one of the many people who actually believe that masturbation is dangerous, you may find that "normal" sexual activities frighten and confuse you. To be seen as unadventurous or inhibited can easily be as embarrassing and painful as to realize that something you believed and lived by for years was in fact completely mythical.

You should face the fact that both you and your partner may have some ideas about sex based on half-truths and other people's ignorance. This does not mean, however, that you should simply accept another's sexual preferences as necessarily right for you.

OPENING UP FOR INTIMACY

Once you have decided that you can speak of your fears or dissatisfaction to your partner, it is important that neither of you confuse attitudes that you may have about sexual intimacy with attitudes about each other. For

Julia and Paul *(see pages 118–121)*, the problems arose when Julia finally voiced a dislike for certain sexual behavior which had become the norm in their lives. In Paul's own words, he "felt slapped in the face" by Julia's revelations. Fortunately Julia meant a great deal to him, so he rightly chose to dig deeper and gently question her feelings.

TRUST AND SEX

Speaking openly about attitudes to sex can be very difficult. For most people, sex is something that is rarely talked about except to closest friends, so the leap of faith needed to confide in a partner can be extreme. It is important that the partner who feels strong in this situation should be open to the other's possibly less confident feelings.

The arousal achieved through wild and passionate sex is not necessarily more stimulating than that found through gentle and romantic loving. Sometimes, too, certain stimulation you discarded years ago as unfulfilling may take on a completely different role now that you are older and seriously involved with your partner.

TRUSTING YOUR PARTNER

For any relationship to be secure it is vital that there is trust between partners. If one partner feels that the other may ridicule or judge his or her feelings it will be harder still for that partner to voice any fears. Or a partner may feel that his or her sexual insecurity or inexperience will color a lover's attitude to other aspects of the relationship—"You're not capable in bed, how can you be trusted with paying the phone bill?" Sometimes, talking through sexual beliefs, or misbeliefs, with a sensitive partner can be the start of a kind of sexual reawakening.

THE JOY OF INTIMACY

Feeling secure with your partner can give you a solid foundation from which you can both blossom. When you know that your partner supports you, you may find it easier to offer support in return. This mutual understanding can take physical and social attraction to a sublime level. Caring for each other's happiness and physical well-being will encompass your mental and emotional strength, too. When you and your partner reach a level of comfortable intimacy, just a glance or a smile can boost and cement your feelings of contentment.

Note, however, that trust also needs to be maintained. You should take the time to confide in each other and make your partner feel special and important. If this sort of environment is maintained, it will be hard for intimacy, and love, not to flourish.

THE "RIGHT" CLIMAX?
Research by Alfred Kinsey in 1953 and Shere Hite in 1978 showed that some 82 percent of women climax during masturbation, while only 30 percent do so during intercourse.

INTIMATE TOUCH
Paul and Julia (see pages 118–121) had to work through their differing attitudes about sex to arrive at a happy medium.

A CONFLICT OF ATTITUDES

Some people love the hot, sticky messiness of sex; others believe that lovemaking should be pure and cerebral. Everybody is entitled to their own opinions, but when these opposites meet up, as with Paul and Julia, life gets emotionally messy, too.

TOO MUCH, TOO SOON

Sometimes a partner seems prissy, snobbish, or just plain choosy when it comes to sex. Earlier therapy (*see pages 28–31*) had worked on Julia's anxieties about sex, but it seemed that, encouraged by the progress Julia had made, Paul was rushing her to accept too much too soon.

NEW PROBLEM

It was Paul who dragged an unwilling Julia to my office. "I love Julia and I know that she loves me," Paul said. "The only thing wrong is bed. We thought we'd gotten over Julia's fears, but now there's a new problem. I adore the rich, sweaty slipperiness of love-making, rolling around in all the juices. The trouble is that Julia hates it."

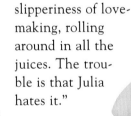

NOT LADYLIKE

"Julia has been struggling to accommodate this side of me, until last week when she couldn't contain herself anymore and burst out that she hates the mess of it. I felt as if I'd been slapped in the face—it's such an integral part of love-making for me. Julia thinks she ought to look ladylike during sex! We've got to put some work in on this—I can't stand the conflict."

Julia's ideas about what made for good sex were different from Paul's

DOING IT HIS WAY

Beneath Julia's newfound air of self-possession, she was still very nervous. "I enjoy sex just as much as Paul does. It's just that I see it as something beautiful. Good sex for me is romantic, gentle, adoring. Paul's liking for all that mess practically amounts to a fetish. I'm not so stupid I don't expect sex to vary. But the trouble is, it's all being conducted the way he wants, never how I'd like it."

CASE NOTES

■

JULIA AND PAUL

Julia's dislike of physical messiness could just have been another aspect of her anxious personality (see pages 28–31), but it is by no means an uncommon aversion. The solution, as often happens when attitudes are in conflict, was to agree on a compromise. Once they had decided on this course of action, Julia and Paul found that the simple exercise for reducing inhibition (see page 122) helped them work out a series of practical actions that both could accept and work with.

Overcoming Dislikes

•

Sexual inexperience sometimes shows up as sexual inhibition. In Julia's case she didn't like to admit she knew so little. Julia needed to get used to the "messiness" of sex—but in her own time, and Paul needed help in slowing down.

TAKING CHARGE

Paul knew Julia's history well, and her excellent progress over the previous months showed that she was capable of change, provided she was offered the right encouragement. For this reason, Julia would benefit from taking charge of lovemaking as long as Paul would go along with this.

Julia took the lead in lovemaking and showed Paul how she liked to be touched

LEARNING TO RELAX

In this way, Julia could get comfortable with her bodily secretions and Paul's at her own speed, just as she'd done previously with her genitals (*see pages 28–31*). Meanwhile, Paul learned to take a more romantic approach to lovemaking.

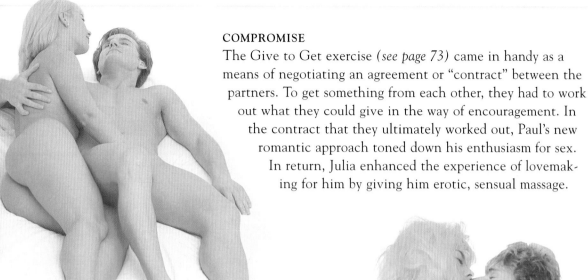

COMPROMISE

The Give to Get exercise (*see page 73*) came in handy as a means of negotiating an agreement or "contract" between the partners. To get something from each other, they had to work out what they could give in the way of encouragement. In the contract that they ultimately worked out, Paul's new romantic approach toned down his enthusiasm for sex. In return, Julia enhanced the experience of lovemaking for him by giving him erotic, sensual massage.

Using erotic massage, Julia gradually became more comfortable with Paul's body

Taking lovemaking more slowly added to Paul and Julia's passion

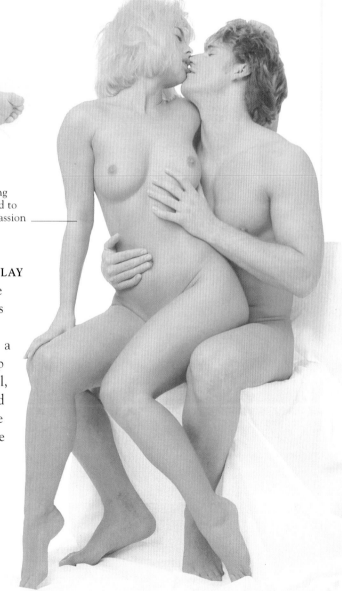

EXTENDED FOREPLAY

Julia learned to use massage techniques (*see pages 101 and 106*) that provided a slow, erotic buildup to intercourse. Paul, meanwhile, learned to spend more time on foreplay than he had before. In this way, what Julia thought of as the "messy" aspect of sex became a less dominant part of lovemaking as a whole. This helped her to overcome her dislike of it, or at least to see lovemaking as superior to it.

ACTION PLAN

SEXUAL INTIMACY cannot be hurried. You may be able to feel extremely close through sexual activity together, but if you rush this, your actions have the opposite effect – they freeze your feelings. What's more, your intimacy isn't only about sex – it's about being open, exposed, and trusting. It may feel risky being so vulnerable, which is why it's a good idea to take things slowly.

SMALL MOVES

The ideal state of intimacy is to feel you've reached the stage where you're able to say or do things that may be difficult for your partner to accept. All this must be done on an equal basis. There can't be double standards here or the action plan doesn't work. For increased sexual intimacy, try some of the following:

- *Stroke your partner in bed.*
- *Say "I love you," or "I think you're wonderful/sexy/attractive" (mental strokes).*
- *Ask your partner to give you mental strokes in a similar way.*
- *Stroke yourself sensuously after a warm bath.*
- *Caress your partner while lying on the side opposite to your usual one in bed. This means using the other hand than you normally do.*
- *Caress yourself during intercourse.*
- *Caress your partner's genitals during intercourse.*
- *Carry out mutual massage (see pages 100–101).*

Intimacy is not only about making sexual moves. Being emotionally closer to your partner can bring about an environment where mutual care and respect have a very positive effect on your sex life and your relationship as a whole. If you want to improve your relationship in this way and feel closer to your partner emotionally, think about implementing the following:

- *Tell your partner what you really want for the future and discuss how you can work toward this together.*
- *Reorganize your family/home life so that you have more freedom to do some of the things you haven't yet achieved.*
- *Go back to school if a complete change seems desirable, and support your partner if he or she also feels such a need.*

Once you've established that you and your partner relate to each other openly and honestly, make sure you respect the trust your partner's honesty places in you.

REDUCING INHIBITION

The aim of this following exercise is to create an upward spiral of improved feeling between you and your partner. Most human beings respond extemely well to care and kindness and wish to reciprocate. If, however, you give and your partner just takes, without offering anything in return, then the overall picture changes. This balance is an unhealthy one and, should your partner prove incapable of meeting you some of the way, you may need to reconsider the relationship.

Above all, keep talking. The more you reveal of yourself and discover about your partner, the closer you are likely to become. If your partner is very inhibited, you might try:

- *Making love in the dark, or at least in dim lighting.*
- *Taking new moves slowly and by degrees. Build up to new activities session by session.*
- *Encouraging the inhibited partner to use assertion techniques (see page 78 for the Yes/No exercise).*
- *Doing the Give to Get exercise (see page 73).*

The Give to Get exercise is based on the principle that if you give people words and actions to make them happy, then they are more likely to feel good about you and will reciprocate.

STRONG EMOTIONS

———————— ■ ————————

If your partner suffers extreme emotional change, helping him or her back to stability can be difficult. Understanding his or her feelings, and the circumstances that led to them, can make it easier to help.

COPING WITH EACH OTHER'S EMOTIONS

Change of any sort unsettles. And change comes in many forms. There's disaster, where life and limb are threatened. There's inner growth, where your outlook on life changes (but often your partner's doesn't). There's physical upheaval, such as moving, which is rated as one of the highest stresses an individual faces. There's also getting laid off, pregnancy, and even vacations.

Any significant change in the usual comfortable pace of life affects our temperament. Gaining a basic understanding that marriage isn't always happy but that if you bear with each other, tolerating the mood swings that emanate from life's upheavals, then you've got a good chance of loving each other forever.

Changes, of course, mean disruption and create powerful passions that have to be dealt with. This chapter, therefore, deals with four of the strongest emotions any of us have to endure. Anger and depression are opposite sides of the same coin and can be frightening both for the person experiencing them and the poor old partner on the receiving end. Jealousy and grief, on the other hand, are especially relevant to love.

Intimacy, sexual and otherwise, is naturally deeply affected by these passions, sometimes with surprising repercussions. But the passions themselves can change your outlook on the world. There's something about being extremely aroused or very despairing that opens us up to change. Many counselors describe a nervous breakdown as a nervous breakthrough, because depressed feelings tell us that something has got to give even if it takes a breakdown to make it possible. Very few people are the same afterward, which is something a partner has to accept—not an easy task.

LONG-TERM DISTRESS
It is rarely a good idea when you're very distressed to dump your feelings on a partner. Although talking difficulties through is at the basis of good communication, it can be deadly to swamp a partner day after day with grief that you have become mired in.

Of course, we should all start off trying to get feelings across to a partner and, in turn, listening to his or hers. But this needs to be gauged carefully. In the section on dealing with anger, a talking task is outlined that can be applied to any difficulty you get obsessed with. It helps you to control how overwhelming the obsession gets. This isn't to say you shouldn't talk to someone else instead. Good friends are invaluable as confidantes and so, of course, are counselors. It's common for counselors to see new clients who explain that they can't continue whining to their friends because their friends are getting sick of them. And yet they have a need to whine.

These people can be dealt with in two ways. First, the expression of grief is important, but so is looking at why some people need to prolong their sorrows. At that stage they are injuring themselves; they are no longer being injured by the original event. This does not discount deep emotional wounds—something very traumatic needs to be relived. But the chance to express this trauma fully, and feel someone has understood, can make a terrific improvement. We may never be the same after a trauma, of course, but we can become, and learn to enjoy being, someone different. And there are very few reasons why that different person can't enjoy many aspects of life.

FORGING CLOSER BONDS

This is where a loving partner comes in. It is possible, by getting through something sad or something infuriating, to forge new bonds. Some people discover that intimacy improves precisely because they've survived difficulties together. The real dangers do not in fact lie in the emotional dilemmas you face, but in simply growing apart to such a degree that you live very separate lives. In those circumstances intimacy fades—it can't help itself, there's nothing to keep it vibrant and alive.

One of the main reasons for this book is to give people practical methods of forging emotional bonds that survive sad occasions. It is not necessarily the case that relationships should be maintained at all costs. But it can be very useful to set yourself internal time limits for just how long you can reasonably last out a difficult relationship before it begins to get unhealthy for you. It's surprising sometimes how just being there for a loved partner helps him or her to improve. And it's also surprising how resilient two people can be after something terrible has happened. So above all, give yourselves time, and if you're hit by an unexpected crisis, try to be supportive.

Often couples find that they gain more intimacy after they survive a sad or traumatic event than in the years beforehand. The way in which they draw together over such tragic situations as, for example, the death of a baby, gives each of them a massive sense of reassurance and trust in themselves, and in their mutual strength.

POSITIVE STEPS
Recovering from, or avoiding, the problems caused by strong or aggressive emotions can bring a couple closer together.

ANGER

A feeling of anger affects us sexually in a complicated fashion. When anger is relatively new it can be exciting and sexy. Even though you've just shouted and screamed at each other you can still get turned on. In fact, all that fighting can actually raise arousal levels, and thus predispose you to some sizzling sex. It is an old idea, but nevertheless a true one, that some of the best times are to be had when making up after an argument.

MAKING PROGRESS
For any good to come from a fight, there have to be working solutions and negotiation. Take you partner's point of view and try to figure out how you can please both of you. Once you have made an agreement you must stick to it—if you don't, the exercise will have been a waste of time for both of you.

Unresolved anger, however, eats away at your feelings and relationship. It can begin to affect the love and respect you have for your partner and can cause radical changes in temperament. It is far more important for the good of your relationship to allow your anger release.

Such long-term anger can affect willingness to compromise and make amends. If it is left long enough it can form a silent barrier where the angry partner sabotages the other on every possible occasion. In other words, if you don't deal with anger, it can permanently damage your relationship.

ALLOWING COMBAT
In order to combat hostility, whether expressed or otherwise, the lines of communication between partners have to be wide open. In other words, there must be a showdown. You cannot expect to solve anything without making it clear what the grievances are. You can forget about any agendas until you have gone through the first confrontation. It's the only way you have of demonstrating that you know that there are problems and that you care about them.

The resolution of anger can be a difficult process, but without resolution anger can damage your relationship.

If you can't do this initially, nothing can be put right. The mechanics of the first exchange are therefore crucial. For your first exchange, at least, you should ensure that the time you allow is an open-ended period, not a snatched fifteen minutes, and not while either of you is otherwise engaged. Be prepared to spend time on this—as much as several hours.

Second, it is important that you are both comfortable with the situation. Don't open your heart in front of other people, especially if your partner will feel that the third party may be taking sides against him or her. In order to draw your partner out you must be prepared to be assertive, but be careful.

Do not confuse assertiveness with aggression. Being assertive means being clear, straight to the point, and sure about what you are saying; it is not a form of verbal attack. Be direct, open, and honest, but sympathetic.

YOUR PARTNER'S REACTION

If your partner reacts to confrontation with anger, swearing, shouting, or screaming, try not to put up any self-defense. Rather than responding defensively, ask your partner if there is more to say. Anything else that must be said? Invite your partner to release all the anger he or she may have. Draw everything out until you encourage your partner to run out of steam. This may prove cathartic, provided you don't interrupt and argue.

In such situations, make sure you don't sound condescending, and do try hard to vary the way you draw your partner out. Arguments can be very productive, but they can take a long time to work through. This is why it is very important for you to have open-ended time. It's not easy just to stand there and let someone be mad at you. Undoubtedly, the temptation to defend yourself or to retaliate is very strong, yet you must resist this temptation if the anger is to be used positively.

YOUR ATTITUDE TOWARD ANGER

Three major qualities are called for in this situation: sincerity, warmth, and empathy. Spontaneity also helps, but it can be difficult when you're feeling bored at having to go through a wearing emotional experience. Yet it's not impossible. Of course, someone else's anger can spark your own. Naturally, an onslaught will trigger your own defenses. For this reason, see the occasion as your partner's catharsis, not yours. If you have anger, express it on another occasion, not this one.

As with any problem-solving conversation there needs to be discussion, negotiation, and compromise, then taking action. Once the tirade is over, don't leap in and take advantage. The person who's sounded off has to keep face. If you were standing when the argument erupted, sit down. By doing so you are putting yourself in a submissive position; you are allowing your partner to have an advantage over you.

REMEMBER TO NEGOTIATE

The catharsis is fine, but in these situations it's simply not enough. It is important that you remember, even in the face of extreme anger, that your partner is hurt and upset and that it's highly likely that he or she does want to work out a solution; otherwise, why expend such energy and emotion? You should also remember, however, that any solution must be practical and within your reach.

ANGER AND PASSION
When confrontation and anger fuel a couple's sex life, any problems may well be hidden in the heat of every moment. For Alice and Matt (see pages 128–131) the time had come for change.

ADDICTED TO ANGER

Sexual reactions to anger are surprisingly varied, and some people get so turned on by anger that they become addicted. Was that what was happening to Alice and Matt? Their relationship was exceptionally fiery and sexy, yet neither liked the other this way.

For Matt and Alice, having a good fight had become a sort of foreplay

FIGHTING AND LOVING

Alice and Matt were each other's first lovers and had been living together for just over six years. They described themselves as being extremely sexual and spent most evenings fighting and making love like crazy. Much as they enjoyed the drama of their passionate relationship, neither enjoyed feeling guilty or slightly disgusted after the arguments and the sex.

DIFFERENT REACTIONS

"The fights blow up out of nowhere until we become completely incandescent with rage," said Matt. "Then we have different reactions. I get completely turned off, but Alice becomes very upset and implores me to make love. I let myself be drawn into this."

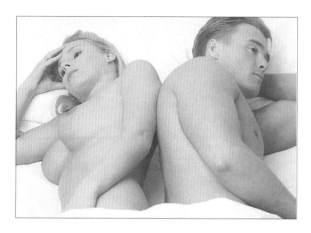

FEELING BAD

"After we've finished," Matt continued, "we both feel as if there's nowhere to go. It doesn't seem natural." Alice agreed. "I find myself feeling really depressed after the fights and the sex," she said. "And I can't imagine, at those times, how we can stay together, with such nothingness between us."

HOOKED ON ROWS

"I'm starting to think we've somehow become hooked on fights as part of our sexual foreplay," said Alice. "I find myself needling Matt for no real reason. He's a great guy and I find him so attractive there are times when I'd like to crawl inside him."

CASE NOTES

ALICE AND MATT

The outward display of anger doesn't always indicate that there are deep-seated personal problems, nor that life is especially stressful. Many people find that emotional arousal, such as that caused by anger, leads to sexual arousal. Some get turned on by the excitement that an argument can create, and then enjoy using lovemaking to release the emotional tension that has built up.

Such behavior is not a problem unless it becomes addictive, as it did for Alice and Matt, but anger that reflects a genuine grievance should always be treated seriously (see page 132).

Finding new outlets for pent-up energy and changing the focus of their relationship by incorporating other interests worked well for Alice and Matt. Their new interests allowed them to concentrate on the calmer aspects of their relationship, and their lovemaking improved because it, too, calmed down.

Breaking the Habit

Alice and Matt needed to find a way to break out of their repetitive cycle of argument followed by lovemaking, which had become almost a routine. Once they had identified the underlying cause of the anger, they were able to replace it with a more constructive pattern of lovemaking.

UNPROVOKED ATTACKS

During counseling sessions, Alice enlarged upon her remark about the fights being a kind of foreplay. She confessed that it was she who instigated them and that she would do so at perfectly ordinary times, such as when they were reading, watching television, or even lying quietly in bed. Outwardly, at least, Matt would have done nothing to provoke her attacks. When asked what was going on in other aspects of her life, her answer was "Very little." The couple hardly ever went out and their best friends lived miles away.

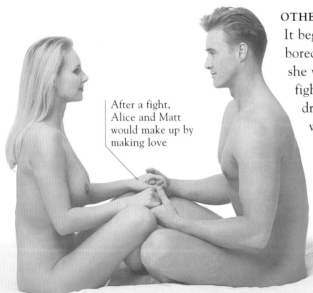

After a fight, Alice and Matt would make up by making love

OTHER INTERESTS

It began to look as if Alice's real problem was boredom. She agreed, and conceded that maybe she was relieving her boredom by instigating fights with her partner in order to enjoy the drama of making up. But Matt was right. It wasn't a healthy pattern of behavior. The solution to the couple's problem was for them to develop other interests so that their minds were stimulated. The first move was to agree on a pact in which sex was seen as a reward for keeping the peace.

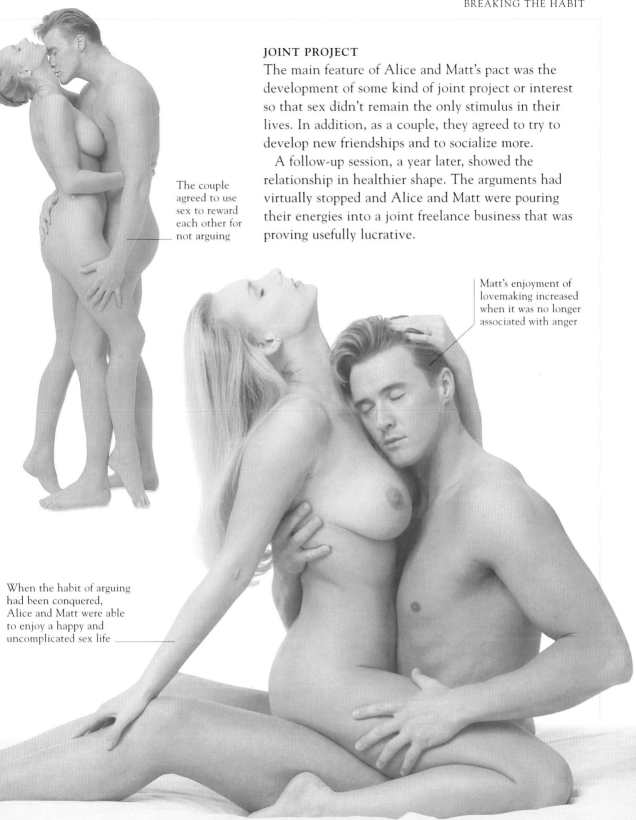

JOINT PROJECT

The main feature of Alice and Matt's pact was the development of some kind of joint project or interest so that sex didn't remain the only stimulus in their lives. In addition, as a couple, they agreed to try to develop new friendships and to socialize more.

A follow-up session, a year later, showed the relationship in healthier shape. The arguments had virtually stopped and Alice and Matt were pouring their energies into a joint freelance business that was proving usefully lucrative.

The couple agreed to use sex to reward each other for not arguing

Matt's enjoyment of lovemaking increased when it was no longer associated with anger

When the habit of arguing had been conquered, Alice and Matt were able to enjoy a happy and uncomplicated sex life

DEALING WITH ANGER

Fights may be cathartic, but unless the dangers exposed by them are dealt with, there will only be a lull before the next storm. There is no point, however, in trying to make changes that are not realistic. So stick with what you are sure you can achieve.

Begin with self-disclosure
or by offering reassurance

Invite your partner to
respond and to explain
his or her problem

Reply to what your
partner has said

Negotiate a solution
to the problem

RESOLVING A PARTNER'S ANGER
Here are four basic steps that can help you face your partner's rage, no matter what the cause.

Before you begin, it is vital to let your partner know that any changes you would like are intended to be constructive and to strengthen your relationship, and that any changes suggested by your partner ought to be so, too. This reassurance can sometimes be hard to offer, but has to be there; if it's not, your partner won't be able to come clean. For the relationship to work well again, you must both be able to talk about what is really worrying you and to make specific and mutually acceptable changes. It is pointless trying to resolve a problem without being prepared to make changes.

OPENING THE DISCUSSION

When you want to discuss whatever it is that is making your partner angry, don't launch straight into the discussion—first spend a little time preparing for it. To begin with, make sure you are approaching the discussion in the right frame of mind. It is not a good idea to fake caring and spontaneity, because such fakery is usually very apparent. Similarly, it is not a time to "suck up" to your partner. And if you are feeling hostile toward your partner because of his or her anger, bear in mind that your goal is to make the relationship work, not to damage it, and you should make that perfectly clear to yourself as well as to your partner.

This preparation should take no more than ten to 15 minutes, because it's vital to get to the heart of the matter without undue delay. Starting the discussion with an item of self-disclosure can be effective, because it shows that you are human and not the monster your partner may have come to see you as. For example, if you say something like: "I know I haven't been doing my fair share of the housework recently," you should follow it up with an invitation to respond, such as, "Is there anything you want to say about it? I'd like to hear it, if there is."

Another good way to begin is by giving your partner reassurance, perhaps by saying something like, "I care about you very much. It makes me unhappy to see you unhappy, and I'm willing to make a lot of changes to improve things between us, which is why I want to be open with you." Having broached the subject, you should encourage your partner to explain his or her side of the problem. Get your partner to express his or her opinions in a brief, direct way with emphasis on the feelings coming from "I" so that it is not simply a list of accusations aimed at "You."

For example, if your partner is angry because your desire for sex conflicts with his or her need for sleep, he or she may say, "I'm fed up with you waking me every night. I need sleep if I'm going to be able to go to work, but when you wake me up, I lie awake for hours. I feel like you're doing it on purpose." When your partner expresses these opinions, you, having listened carefully, should explain your view of the situation. Then the two of you can negotiate a solution to the problem (see page 72).

UNRESOLVED ANGER
There may come a time when no amount of talking is going to solve the problem—for example, if one of you has done something unforgivable. Sometimes the only feasible resolution to such confrontation is splitting up. For instance, if a woman finds out that her partner is having an affair with her sister, that's likely to mean the end of the relationship. But if she can see that the infidelity was merely a symptom of something wrong in the relationship, and that the choice of lover was incidental, then there's still something left to work on.

FACING ANGER
Comfort after angry words is important for apologies and forgiveness.

DEALING WITH ANGER

When facing your partner's anger, any discussion will be far more productive if you try to follow a few simple rules. Before you begin, acknowledge your partner's anger as something that is important to both of you, and try to hold on to that view throughout your confrontation.

1 Be warm and genuine, don't be patronizing, and use no subterfuge.

2 Combine warmth with empathy to show your sincerity.

3 Employ good listening techniques (see page 66).

4 Pick up on what your partner is thinking and feeling (see page 66).

5 Don't adopt an interrogator's stance.

An interrogator typically sits directly in front of his or her victim and leans forward, intently watching for any flicker of emotion that might betray hidden secrets. That kind of approach instantly creates feelings of paranoia, resentment, defensiveness, and mistrust in the person in the hot seat. This will only fuel your partner's anger, and if it stems from other feelings of resentment, it is unlikely that you will resolve the situation.

Once you have established the cause of your partner's anger, the two of you can begin negotiations for a solution, or at least attempt to work out a way in which the situation will be avoided in the future.

DEPRESSION

Feelings of diminished sexuality and depression are closely entwined. Like the chicken and the egg, it can be difficult to know which leads to the other. Undoubtedly the quality of your sex life is affected by how happy or depressed you are, and this can be the culmination of the stresses and strains of a number of life events, from overwork to hormonal and physical causes.

When you are put under a lot of pressure in your life, your reaction can incorporate many responses. You may feel emotionally muted, as if you are reacting to the world through layers of cotton. This can make you feel that you're not really part of things and have no impact or worth. Then there's the sort of strain that makes sufferers feel as though they are going to burst. The pressure builds up until it becomes impossible to relieve and nothing seems to come easily. After prolonged pressure like this a person may begin to feel that sanity is hanging by a thread. And finally there's breakdown, when strain and depression are so acute that nothing escapes unaffected and life itself feels like a burden. This is so extreme it can, in some cases, lead to a total shutdown of a person's ability to interact with the world.

If the stresses of life become too much, the ensuing depression can affect all aspects of your life, including sex.

ARE THERE MANY SUFFERERS?

Depression is twice as common as heart disease and three times as prevalent as cancer. Twice as many women as men are victims, and the rate is three times higher for mothers. As many as 55 percent of the population admit to having some form of depression—the rest are either plain lucky or simply hide their difficulties.

WHAT IS SEXUAL DEPRESSION?

Lack of interest in sex is a common symptom of depression and may often show what is really going on inside a person. The term "sexual depression" in this context means a lessened or even total lack of interest in sex caused by feelings of depression. Sex is such a complicated emotional and physical interaction, yet loss of sex drive is often seen as something wrong with the relationship. In fact, this loss can have many causes other than loss of interest in a partner. It may be, for example, that the bedroom is one of the few places where a person can take control.

MAKING CHANGES

Psychologist Dorothy Rowe says that "on the scale of human suffering, the experience of depression is among the most immense.... No matter how great our physical pain may be, it is possible to feel close and loving to those around us, to let their love and comfort come through to us, and warm and succor us. But in depression we cannot separate ourselves from our misery nor can we draw close to people, for we become locked in a prison which love cannot penetrate."

It can be very difficult for a person to understand that his or her partner is suffering from depression. If you notice that your partner is becoming more and more withdrawn, tearful, sleepless, and restless, it is all too easy to assume that there is a problem in your relationship. It is far better to take the view that it is only because your relationship is stable that your partner feels the freedom to relieve his or her stresses in your company.

This concept may seem rather idealistic, but unless you show positive strength your partner will see the relationship with you as another area of difficulty and stress in an already overburdened life. It is also very difficult to deal with a partner who is in pain but shows no outward signs of being hurt. With depression, there are no markers by which you can judge the extent of your partner's illness, nor the recovery. The good news is that depression can be beaten, and most people will recover fully. But this requires a great deal of support and understanding on the parts of those around the sufferer, especially from his or her partner.

WHAT LEADS TO SEXUAL DEPRESSION?

Unavoidable situations in your life, such as the death of a loved one or having too much work to do, can lead to a growing feeling that you are unable to cope and that everything is too difficult. This in turn can bring about a loss of interest in sex.

Common causes of depression, and sexual depression, include stressful life events such as bereavement, separation and divorce, unemployment, changing jobs, and moving. Also, life stages such as adolescence and menopause, where fluctuating hormone levels are the cause, can be added to this list. Furthermore, other events that involve hormonal changes—including premenstrual tension, postpartum depression, and sometimes impotence—can cause depression, while poor health (generally poor health or a chronic condition) and some aftereffects of surgery can have a very negative effect.

Certain drugs, such as tranquilizers, antihistamines, and drugs to control blood lipids and blood pressure, may also reduce sexual desire. Depression can lead to feelings of personal inadequacy and discomfort with others, even your partner. In turn, he or she may see this as a cooling of your feelings, and feel rejected, and may therefore inadvertently add pressure by seeking reassurance when you are not strong enough to give it.

STRESSFUL LIVES
Maria (see pages 136–139) was relieved that Julio's diminished feelings were not caused by loss of interest in her.

A LACK OF DESIRE

Anxiety and depression can kill sexuality. For Julio, a fear of going broke had turned him off lovemaking. Unfortunately, his wife Maria believed that she was at fault, but trying to arouse Julio by dressing up in sexy black underwear hadn't been the answer.

TAKING THE BLAME

It's a common assumption that you must be doing something wrong if your man loses interest in sex. Maria believed that she had somehow lost her powers of attraction for Julio, her husband. Since therapy for Julio's verbal bullying (*see pages 62–65*), they had enjoyed good and loving sex. "Now," she said, "I'm lucky if he makes love to me every six weeks, and even then I have to coax and cajole him."

FEAR

"I'm so afraid that he doesn't desire me anymore," Maria sobbed. "I've wondered if there's another woman, but he swears not. He says that he's just too tired to make love and has things on his mind. These days I actually dress up to go to bed. The black stockings and garter belt were what he found most provocative."

WORRIES

Julio refused to accompany his wife to counseling, so she was able to talk freely. She explained that she and her husband were very close and intimate but that recently her husband had been worried that his business was failing. He'd been desperately trying to improve sales, knowing that the business might fold. The livelihood of several members of his family depended on the company. "I've done my best to be supportive," said Maria.

REJECTION

She explained that things had reached the stage where she was now feeling very unloved and rejected. "Suddenly, Julio won't talk about anything—he absolutely refuses. But I've got to sort something out because otherwise I'm going to go crazy. I know it's a bad time to force him into talking, because he's got such worries about the business. But what else can I do?"

CASE NOTES

MARIA AND JULIO

Depression takes many forms. But one way in which it commonly shows up is in loss of sexual desire. By bottling up his feelings, Julio increased his depression— but Maria saw only his lack of sexual interest. She had no insight into his worries.

Maria truly believed that Julio was no longer attracted to her, but could not figure out why. When she realized that worries over work were causing him to feel depressed, she was able to act. Offering Julio support at home and refraining from adding to the pressures in his life helped her to steer their relationship—and Julio's sex drive—back on course.

Counseling helped examine the causes of his depression and, more importantly, showed them how to deal with them (see page 140).

It can be very upsetting for your partner if your worries mean you fail to acknowledge the love that is offered to you

Rekindling Desire

*For Maria, one of the most distressing aspects of Julio's lack of
sexual desire was that she blamed herself for it. But through
talking it over in counseling, she soon understood
the problem. Armed with that knowledge, she
began to rebuild their relationship.*

FINDING THE CAUSE

When Maria began to examine other problem
areas, a more complete picture emerged of the
difficulties Julio was having with his general
health. He couldn't sleep, kept waking during
the night, had obsessive worries that churned
around his head, felt exhausted, and was eating
little. In other words, he was exhibiting classic
signs of depression. Lack of sexual desire is
often one of the many areas affected.

POSITIVE ACTION

Maria was greatly relieved to learn that the decline in their
sex life was not because her attractions were diminishing,
and she expressed her willingness to do absolutely
anything she could that would help her husband.
On the grounds that sharing worries often helps a
worrier feel better, Maria agreed to encourage
Julio to talk more.

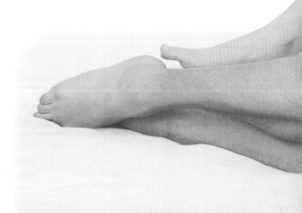

LIGHTENING THE LOAD

Since Julio wouldn't attend counseling or even go to the doctor to check on his symptoms, Maria would need to be completely self-motivating. She acted by telling him that he could rely on her to do anything to help and did everything practical in the house to take pressure off his shoulders. Furthermore, she desisted from asking for or pressuring him about sex. This didn't mean, however, that she stopped showing him in every way that she still found him attractive and that she loved him dearly. It's not easy lasting out someone else's depression when he or she refuses to seek help.

RETURN TO INTIMACY

Through her love and concern for her husband, Maria developed patience and never doubted that the situation would improve. Julio's business did eventually pull through the crisis and Maria could virtually gauge the improvement by the subsequent return of her husband's sexual desire.

It is a wonderful feeling when your partner's worries are replaced by the return of desire

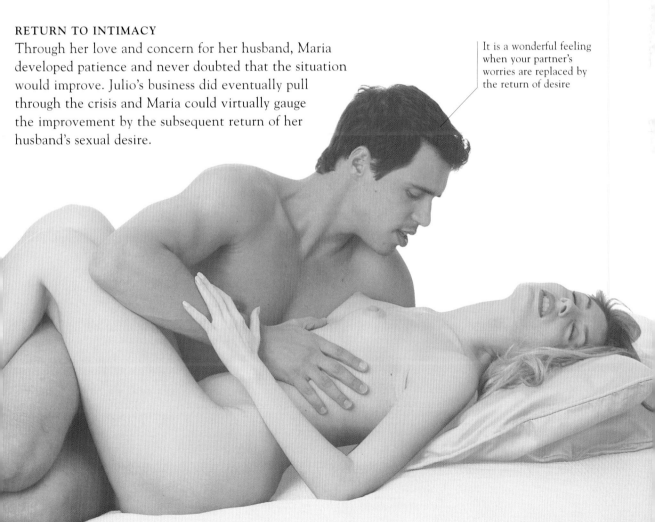

BEATING DEPRESSION

Have you ever felt so helpless that you were unable to cope with simple tasks? Did the anticipation of a meeting fill you with dread? Did you see yourself as incapable of contributing, or feel that you would never be strong again? If you answer "yes" to any of these you may also know the importance of taking positive action to understand, combat, and recover from depression.

MILD DEPRESSION
Anxiety, moodiness, tearfulness, tiredness, irritability, inability to concentrate

MODERATE DEPRESSION
Sleeplessness, loss of appetite and interest in sex, lethargy or agitation

SEVERE DEPRESSION
Guilt, worthlessness, thoughts of death and suicide, hallucinations, delusions

TYPICAL SYMPTOMS OF DEPRESSION
For many people the minor day-to-day worries they face are easily coped with. For others, these worries can become overwhelming, and can lead to far more severe symptoms, even thoughts of suicide.

There are two schools of thought about the best methods for treating depression. One advocates counseling and the use of talking therapies to work through what may be real worries based on real-life events. This can help you to put into perspective those areas of your life that have become too difficult for you to cope with. These may often be areas that you once found challenging and exciting, such as your job or your children.

The other school recommends asking your doctor to prescribe you antidepressants. These benefit over 70 percent of sufferers, and although the positive effects may not last, they provide a short-term relief from depression, which can give a welcome boost to your self-esteem and clarity of thought.

Where the depression is not obviously linked to a life event such as a bereavement, there's a lot to be said for employing both methods. Having lifted the depression with drugs (the newer types of antidepressant are mainly nonaddictive), counseling through the new and improved state of mind can help examine and work on the underlying depressive triggers.

PROTECTIVE DEPRESSION

In some instances a temporary attack of depression may arise in order to "look after" you when you feel threatened by too much change or too many feelings. If you are facing an overload of emotional or mental pressure, your body may simply acknowledge this and force you to take some time off for you to begin to recover your strength.

Perhaps going to bed and pulling the blanket over your head, saying, "I can't face this," is exactly what you need to do in order to face the world refreshed in a few days' time. If your depression lasts longer than this, however, you may need professional help.

As explained previously, some therapists deliberately use the term "nervous breakthrough" rather than the more conventional "nervous breakdown." This is because feelings of depression are one of the ways in which the body tells you that you can no longer cope with the emotions that are being channeled into you. Quite simply, these feelings are telling you that something has to change, even if this takes a breakdown. Few people are completely the same emotionally or mentally after such an event.

SEEKING AND GIVING SUPPORT

This is an example of where the expression of your feelings is so important. As soon as you voice your feelings, you free those feelings for change. Your partner may force you to react by commenting on your feelings. Or you may realize that your partner too has had such feelings and may be able to suggest solutions. Or maybe you simply need someone you trust who will listen. If you worry that your partner sees your feelings as weakness, or you as incompetent because of them, it may be that this is the cause. Having a supportive partner can greatly reduce both anxiety and depression you feel in the relationship.

TEAMWORK
Pressures of depression can divide a couple. Both must then work hard to overcome the problems that arise.

DEALING WITH SEXUAL DEPRESSION

If you suffer from sexual depression, there are several steps you can take to help alleviate the symptoms of the immediate problem. These suggestions are helpful only for relatively mild depression, however, and if any spell of depression becomes acute or persistent, it is vital that you seek medical help as soon as possible.

A woman whose depressive bouts are premenstrual in origin could:
1 Use a menstrual diary to identify the most difficult days of her monthly cycle;
2 Develop a strategy for dealing with these difficult days, for instance, by resolving to try to be more outgoing on those days, or simply accepting she will feel bad;
3 Focus on being strong during the rest of the month;
4 Try to get more exercise and eat healthfully, as this will increase her general well-being, improving her mood and possibly her sex drive.

A man who is worried about depression-related impotence could:
1 Check that there is no underlying physical cause for his symptoms;
2 Reassess his lifestyle to find ways of reducing stress;
3 Practice self-stimulation: unlike intercourse, masturbation involves no real or imagined "pressure to peform," and can build sexual confidence.

If your depression is linked to fears about a relationship, seeking counseling may be the most direct way to find out exactly where you stand with your partner. It will also provide practical methods to help you improve your relationship.

JEALOUSY

"Military leader kills wife in fit of jealousy. Dead woman innocent. Best friend implicated." Are these headlines familiar? They refer to Shakespeare's play Othello, *written some 400 years ago, yet which could just as easily have been written yesterday. But jealousy has been with us for thousands of years, since long before Shakespeare used it for inspiration.*

Ranging from the odd twinge of uncertainty to an uncontrollable and pathological emotional upheaval, jealousy is an enigmatic emotion. Views on jealousy have changed over time. Even as late as the 1970s people were considered sick if they experienced feelings of jealousy. They were exhorted to look within themselves to try to discover just where it was that this supposedly immature emotion was coming from.

Jealousy is a troublesome emotion, but it can be controlled and even used as a source of motivation.

Now, however, most of us no longer believe that a sickness of the mind is responsible for the appearance of the green-eyed monster. Nearly everyone feels jealous at some time. Older children, for example, may be jealous of the newborn younger child, not necessarily because they are opposed to the existence of the younger, only insecure because the parents', especially the mother's, attention is suddenly focused elsewhere. This jealousy tends to be grounded in reality as the parents try to accustom themselves to a new child.

If you suffer this, the way you are helped through depends on how careful and caring your parents are during and after the event. This can be vital to feelings of security for the rest of your life. And the rival need not be a new baby. Perhaps Dad or another relative, such as an elderly grandparent, is seen as taking Mom away and begrudged her attention.

JEALOUSY OUT OF CONTROL

In a situation where your initial suspicions take root, whether they are justified or not, you look for things to confirm them. If you find any such confirmation, your jealousy increases, even when your partner denies all accusations, until you finally reach a point where jealousy becomes the dominant feature of your life.

POSITIVE JEALOUSY

Although jealousy is invariably seen as a negative emotion, it can, in fact, be a source of motivation. In some instances, a twinge of jealousy can revitalize a flagging relationship if you suddenly realize that your partner is attractive to other people. These realizations may spur you to demonstrate your love for your partner, and boost your relationship. Someone else's appreciation of your partner has highlighted areas needing improvement.

DEFICIT JEALOUSY

Claude Steiner, a Californian clinical psychologist, has defined what he terms as "deficit jealousy" which occurs when one partner feels that there is an uneven or unfair balance in marital giving. If, for example, a wife spends all her time nurturing her husband, cooking for him, and ensuring his comfort, she will understandably be irked if he is always too tired to talk to her, ignores her, spends every weekend pursuing his own interests, and is a lazy lover. If the husband then appears to give "nurturing" to his secretary under the guise of working late, his wife is highly likely to become jealous, whether her husband really is working late or not.

Deficit jealousy is relatively easy to deal with. By getting the couple to examine the whole relationship rather than the specific incidents they may be able to think more laterally about their relationship. In a situation like the one above, the wife may be afraid that her marriage will be exposed as weak. Yet, paradoxically, acknowledging such weakness may strengthen and improve the relationship.

REAL FOUNDATIONS FOR JEALOUSY

In many instances there may be entirely rational reasons for a flirtation with the green-eyed monster. If, for example, your partner returns home late on a few occasions and you discover a book of matches from a local hotel, of which he or she swears ignorance, it's reasonable for you to feel suspicious about his or her behavior.

Sometimes these suspicions are not even based on anything as concrete as the matches. Nevertheless, you pick up from this partner you know so well the feeling that something is strange. The changes in behavior may be almost imperceptible, but your finely tuned responses become alert to the fact that something has happened. This reading of your partner is based on instinctive observation of actual, perceptible differences, tiny discrepancies in behavior that, put together, equal the possibility of a rival.

If there are real reasons for you to feel jealous, then it's perfectly reasonable that you do so. A huge chunk of your emotional security is being threatened and you need to defend yourself. These are normal reactions.

PATHOLOGICAL JEALOUSY

There are, sadly, people so locked into their all-consuming jealousy that they find it almost impossible to break out. They are obsessive, anxious and feel compelled to react as they do. Because pathological jealousy is obsessive it is difficult to treat. But the advance of new anti-anxiety and antidepressant drugs, combined with therapy, is proving to be a breakthrough. In such cases medical treatment should be sought.

READING THE SIGNS
Polly's jealousy (see pages 144–147) had foundation. George, her husband, was faltering in the marriage and seeing another woman.

SUSPICION AND GUILT

"Jealousy made me have an affair." Excuse or genuine reason?
This is the debate Polly had when she felt guilty after the event.
Yet it was her husband who had first strayed. Or had he?
Polly didn't know if she was right to be jealous.

USEFUL THERAPY

The trouble with jealousy is that there are at least two sorts. The first is the kind where the jealousy stems from your own insecurity and probably nothing else. The second is when you pick up real clues and are likely to read the truth from them. Polly's problem lay in not really knowing from which sort of jealousy she suffered, and that problem was complicated by her affair. But Polly was sure that she wanted her marriage to work.

One reason for this was that previous therapy (*see pages 46–49*) had helped Polly and George to develop a satisfying sex life, and they both loved their child dearly.

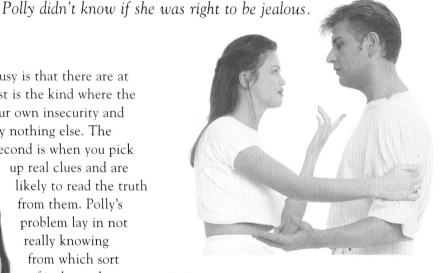

SUSPICION

"I spent months feeling awful about his flirtations," Polly said. "He often came home late and once I picked up the phone and recognized the voice of one of the women he regularly flirted with. I was so jealous I almost attacked him, but he just denied everything."

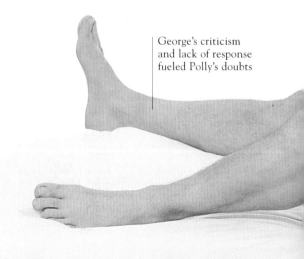

George's criticism and lack of response fueled Polly's doubts

Polly felt guilty about her brief affair

GUILT

"In the end, I accepted the invitation of the next available man," she continued, "and went to bed with him. I felt better afterward but also guilty. I'm not sure, now, that George really was sleeping around. I may have exaggerated his flirtations. I feel uneasy when I think about it."

CASE NOTES

GEORGE AND POLLY

Although Polly's anxiety was almost indefinable, her suspicions about the quality of her marriage turned out to be accurate. George had had an affair, Polly had retaliated by having one of her own, and now George was purposefully making his wife feel inferior.

Working agreements

A major cause of arguments between partners is when one believes that the other is having an affair. Even though they may come to an acceptable working agreement about staying together (see page 148), the hurt or "innocent" partner may need to talk it over many more times. This can be tough on the "guilty" partner, since he or she might be trying to get on with the marriage itself.

HURTFUL CRITICISM

Unfortunately, whether or not George had indeed had an affair, he was making the relationship difficult by constantly putting Polly down, often in front of friends. Although he adored his child, he was highly critical of his wife and, among many other things, slighted her once-exciting bedroom technique.

Setting the Limits

·

When Polly realized how her husband was making her feel inferior and insecure, she was able to assert herself, set limits on his behavior, and make it clear to him that her patience was not inexhaustible. Eventually, these tactics paid off.

INSECURITY

Polly was sensible to seek help, not necessarily because of her jealousy or her affair but because there seemed to be an imbalance in the marriage that allowed George to feel superior and made her feel inferior. This wasn't healthy, and was the basis of Polly's insecurity.

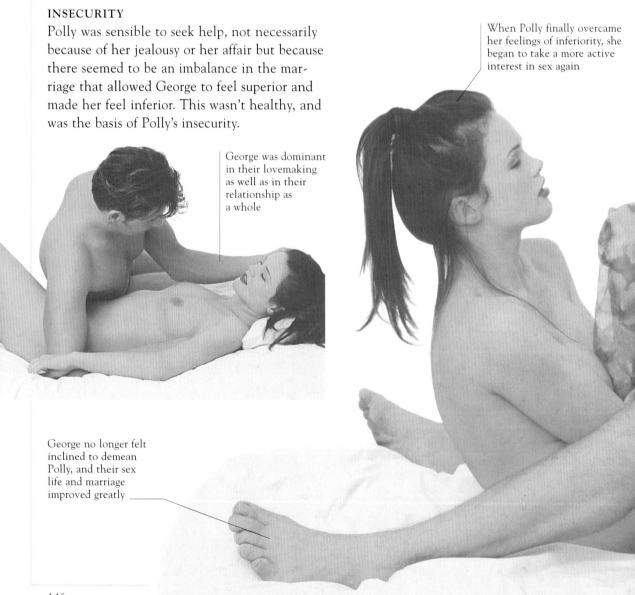

When Polly finally overcame her feelings of inferiority, she began to take a more active interest in sex again

George was dominant in their lovemaking as well as in their relationship as a whole

George no longer felt inclined to demean Polly, and their sex life and marriage improved greatly

ASSERTIVENESS

Polly tackled the problem on two fronts.
First, she vowed to challenge George
every time he was rude. Second, she decided
to explain her feelings. If she always felt inferior, she
would no longer love her husband. Did he really
want this? His initial response was to make peace
with her, but his flirting soon resurfaced when she
discovered he was secretly having an affair.

George's affair added
to his confused
feelings for
——— his wife

George regained
respect and love
for Polly ———

RECONCILIATION

Polly returned to counseling two years later, to
say that George had felt that he was competing
with their child for her affection and had
withdrawn from her. The outcome was that
he had moved in with another woman. But
a few weeks later, George unexpectedly
approached her for reconciliation, realizing that what he had initially loved in
Polly had not waned, and that his family was more important to him than
his new lover. Polly felt the same
way. Fortunately she was able to
see beyond his infidelity, and
she took him back.

DEFEATING JEALOUSY

It is widely agreed that there is a clear link between jealousy and low self-esteem. Partners who feel secure in their relationship, and about themselves, are far less prone to bouts of irrational jealousy. For those who suffered uncertainty and doubt about their partners, it was found that the extent and frequency of these jealous feelings was diminished when they learned to be less dependent and worked on trusting themselves instead.

Discuss the problem
with your partner

Analyze the problem to
discover the true reason
or reasons behind it

Reassure each other that
you will work together to
resolve the problem

Agree on any
necessary action

Implement
the changes

DEALING WITH JEALOUSY
A rational view of jealous feelings can help put them, and the problem areas of your relationship, into perspective.

Clinical psychologist Claude Steiner suggests that if we concentrate on seeing jealousy as an exciting challenge, rather than as something that is negative and fearsome, we may actually be able to solve some of the problems it brings about. He suggests that it is very important for anyone who is suffering feelings of jealousy to acknowledge and question exactly what they signify and where they come from.

APPROACHING JEALOUSY
If your jealous feelings are based on reality you should ask your partner to talk these feelings through with you. Be aware that this conversation may be painful, but it is vital if you are to get to the heart of the matter.

Explain to your partner that you are aware the focus has been taken off your relationship. This may lead you to look at what is not working for your partner in the relationship, what may be triggering his or her feelings of boredom, depression, or stagnation. If things have gone too far for the two of you to unravel on your own, take the difficulties to a therapist for expert help.

HONESTY AND SUPPORT
If your partner feels that you are accusing him or her of infidelity, then you are not voicing your feelings accurately. Instead, you should try to express the need you have for reassurance and be open about your fears, or your partner will never be able to support you. Similarly, if your partner approaches you with feelings of jealousy, try to understand that, to some extent, you too may be at fault for not ensuring your partner's security in your relationship.

If you and your partner find discussions about the feelings behind jealousy painful, be supportive of each other and try to use the pain as an incentive for change—your relationship is worth it.

COPING WITH DEFICIT JEALOUSY

With deficit jealousy it is important that both partners concentrate on relieving the problems behind the jealous feelings, and a give-to-get approach often works well. If a wife feels that her husband is neglecting her in favor of work, a hobby, or other friends, it may be that her outward show of jealousy is pushing him away. If the husband works on making his wife feel more secure, she may become far happier and more approachable. He in turn will feel that he wants to spend more time with her. Thus, both will begin to feel happy and secure in their relationship once more.

HELPING YOURSELF

For all your partner's help, the biggest step to overcoming jealousy is to learn to value yourself. Try to work out ways to strengthen your self-esteem so that you rely less on your partner for good feelings. Don't look to others as a guide for your own abilities, or negate those skills you have.

  If you are dealing with what feels like a near-pathological jealousy problem, psychotherapy, a talking treatment over a long period of time, may well be necessary. Ask your doctor for a referral as drug treatment may be part of the therapy you need.

REGAINING TRUST

It may be hard for your partner to convince you that your jealousy is groundless. Nonetheless, no one else can do it, so you must work together to overcome your fears.

DEALING WITH JEALOUSY

If you can take a rational view of your jealousy it can be very important for your relationship to work out what has caused it. If you pinpoint the reasons, you may discover that insecurities you developed during childhood are the cause. If so, this exercise may help you deal with the jealousy and save your relationship.

1 Talk to your partner about whatever may have given rise to your jealousy.

2 Explore how your relationships during childhood may have affected your inner sense of security and therefore your present outward show of jealous feelings.

3 Ask your partner how he or she would like you to change.

4 Try to establish those changes.

5 Try not to react defensively as soon as you begin to feel jealous.

6 Concentrate on where the jealousy really comes from (that is, your childhood).

7 Work on ways in which your partner could support you in these changes.

8 Accept gentle reminders that your jealousy within the relationship is unfounded.

9 Accept words of appreciation and love to help you to feel valued.

If your partner really wants to help, he or she could bear your feelings in mind and try to temper his or her own reactions at the same time as reassuring you.

This does not mean, however, that your partner should stop behaving normally! It only means that he or she must make a true attempt to understand how hurt you may feel if there is any uncertainty about his or her actions.

GRIEF

"Crazed with grief"—an old-fashioned description but an accurate one. Intense grief is an abnormal state. The sensations may be so overwhelming that they change your bodily functions. It's not unusual, for example, to lose your appetite or, for women, to cease menstruating for a while. Mentally, feelings may prove so acute that sufferers become obsessive and vengeful.

Emotions that are very powerful, such as grief, may well have negative repercussions on your sex life. This is hardly surprising when your hormones are acting unusually. It may be even more difficult if the grief is associated with the death or defection of a lover. It is highly likely that pain, depression, and anger are also mingled here and, in self-defense, your body can block sexual sensation. On the other hand, sexual intercourse can actually be an outlet for pain, with the grieving person seeking sexual solace, often in the arms of a friend or ex-lover.

SYMPTOMS OF GRIEF

The major feeling of grief is loss. We grieve for the loss of anything that matters to us. Often the first sensations to hit are shock and numbness. This, perhaps, is nature's way of protecting us from panic and pain, but after a few days or weeks, a new and far more difficult set of emotions takes over.

Grief is the natural reaction to the loss of a loved one, and an emotion that should be expressed, not stifled.

Initially you may suffer denial and feel unable to accept that the person has gone. When you do realize they're gone you may be so depressed that you feel that there is no way you can cope without them. If a person dies tragically you may get uncontrollably angry with them for having left you, and you may also, reasonably or not, feel guilty and responsible for the death. Despair may set in as you realize that that person is never going to love you again, or that there are things that were left incomplete or unfinished between you.

COPING WITH LOSS

You should allow yourself to cry, to scream, and generally relieve your feelings, and it is important that your partner understands your feelings and accepts your need to grieve in your own way for as long as it takes.

All these symptoms are normal and healthy. Your grief may last many months, even years, and anniversaries and holidays may refresh the feelings that you thought you'd overcome. Eventually, however, you will begin to feel stronger and more able to face living again.

THE SEXUAL COMPONENT

Emotional symptoms can often lead to physical ones. If your problem involves loss of desire, don't be afraid. Sexual feeling does return, but it takes time and patience. Take the precaution of explaining this to your partner so that he or she doesn't read anything personal into it—it can be very difficult for a partner to take second place to someone who is dead, no matter how understanding he or she tries to be. Make maximum use of cuddles and closeness to ensure that you both realize that love and support have not also been lost.

If your partner is grieving and having trouble with sexual drive, respect his or her feelings and be considerate. Don't foist your own demands for gratification onto a suffering bereaved person and try not to add to his or her worries by reacting to any real, or imagined, distance between you.

"FROZEN" GRIEF

Occasionally, bereaved people suffer from an abnormal grief reaction. Perhaps the grief is blocked off completely with the effect that the emotions are put into a sort of deep freeze. This isn't usually a problem for the sufferer, but it may be for his or her partner. Patience and encouragement may eventually trigger a more conventional reaction such as tears and a sense of loss, effectively unblocking the emotions. This will make it easier for the person who is grieving and his or her partner to begin to recover.

COMPULSIVE GRIEF

More rarely, a few people react to grief in a manic fashion. If this is your way of dealing with loss, perhaps you speed up and polish off tasks connected with the departed person, and try to control events and emotions with speed and efficiency. A side of this may be a compulsion for sex.

STARTING AGAIN

If you have lost a partner, it may take you some time to regain the sense of being comfortable in the company of the opposite sex. It is important that you do not feel that you have something to prove. Take these steps at your own speed. If you do find another special person, try to voice your feelings honestly so that, as with Ronnie and Janine (*see pages 152–155*), you face any difficulties together and give each other patient support.

DIVORCE GRIEF
Most people experience divorce as a major loss and feel similar to those who are bereaved. The emotions of divorce grief are less clear-cut than those that arise from someone's death because, in most cases, one partner has deliberately chosen to leave the other.

Some people find that talking to their friends helps them through, while others struggle on alone. Bereavement counseling can help men and women who are "stuck" in grief.

STARTING AGAIN
Ronnie and Janine (see pages 152–155) faced troubled times early in their relationship when Ronnie's grief overshadowed their love.

STARTING AGAIN

If you've remained faithful to one partner all your married life, you can be left with an upsetting problem when he or she dies. Ronnie discovered that even though he wanted to, he couldn't consummate his new relationship with Janine—at the crucial moment, he'd feel guilty.

HEADING
Although Ronnie desired his new partner, Janine, when it came to penetration he lost his erection every time. He had been able to bring Janine to climax with his hands, but he was miserable and worried that he would never again have a complete and fulfilling physical relationship. This was particularly important because his relationship with Janine was helping him recover from the death of his wife, Claire.

IMPAIRED RESPONSE
Grief can affect your sexual response in several ways. Sexual desire may decline or even cease for a time, because you can be so habituated to a partner that, unconsciously, you feel it is wrong to be sexual with anyone else even though you know this to be ridiculous. This was certainly the case for Ronnie.

CASE NOTES

RONNIE AND JANINE

We establish clearly defined patterns of lovemaking in long-term relationships, so sex can feel strange if later you want to make love to someone new. New patterns are, of course, created with new lovers, but Ronnie felt a duty to be faithful to his deceased wife.

A loss of interest in sex is just one way in which the mind of a bereaved person demonstrates, via the body, just how much he or she was attached to the person who died. It is a sign that there is still a need to let go of the sadness inside.

Ronnie needed to give himself time to grieve (see page 156) and to get used to being with his new partner. One way to achieve this was to concentrate on loving but nonpenetrative sex until Ronnie overcame his grief and was ready for intercourse.

FIDELITY

Ronnie, who had previously had counseling with his late wife (*see pages 68–71*), said "Claire's death, of cancer, was a great shock. I didn't have any other sexual partners during our marriage. I didn't want anyone else. Now I'm very attracted to Janine and have all the usual urges, but my body is letting me down."

FEELINGS OF UNFAITHFULNESS

"Janine and I have tried to make love many times," he continued. "But I couldn't manage it. I could start off okay, but at the moment of entry I'd see a vision of Claire and feel as if I were being unfaithful. I know this is ridiculous. Janine has been very patient, so far. I have no problem getting and keeping an erection when I masturbate, so I know that there is nothing wrong with me physically."

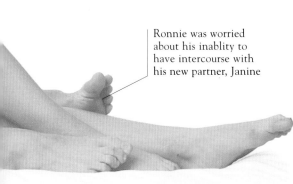

Ronnie was worried about his inablity to have intercourse with his new partner, Janine

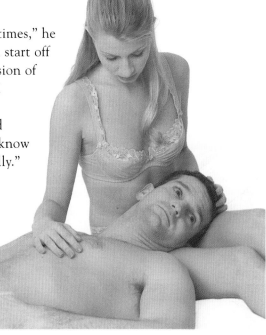

153

Regaining Sexual Happiness

*Naturally, new sexual patterns are created with new lovers, but
for Ronnie these new patterns were being expected of him
far too soon, especially as his original ones had taken
years to establish. Ronnie needed to slow down and
take time to discover his new lover.*

STAYING CLOSE

The couple had, without
realizing it, already begun
to use the kind of non-
penetrative routines—
including sensual touch,
mutual pleasuring, and
self-pleasuring—that
would help them establish
and maintain physical
and emotional closeness.
Extending these intimate
physical routines to
include sexual games and
erotic massage *(see pages
101 and 106)* would help
keep their sex life alive,
active, and enjoyable
until Ronnie was ready
for intercourse.

IMPATIENCE

Ronnie said that his usual style
of lovemaking consisted mainly
of intercourse and that he'd paid
little attention to foreplay. This
suggested impatience. Perhaps he
was trying to consummate his
relationship with Janine before
he was ready.

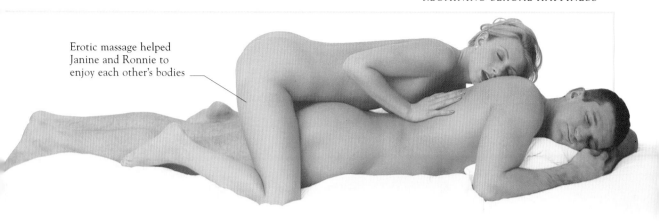

Erotic massage helped
Janine and Ronnie to
enjoy each other's bodies

SENSUAL PLEASURING

Janine readily accepted the suggestion that she
and Ronnie would benefit from turning their
lovemaking into periods of play and sensual
pleasuring. This would help Ronnie relax into
their new sexual patterns.

Ronnie still used
manual and oral
stimulation to
help bring Janine
to climax

BACK TO NORMAL

Within a few months, Ronnie felt ready to try
intercourse again and was delighted and
relieved to discover that his body responded
fully. Although he and Janine relished this
return to intercourse,
they both chose to
continue with the
erotic massage and
sensual pleasuring.

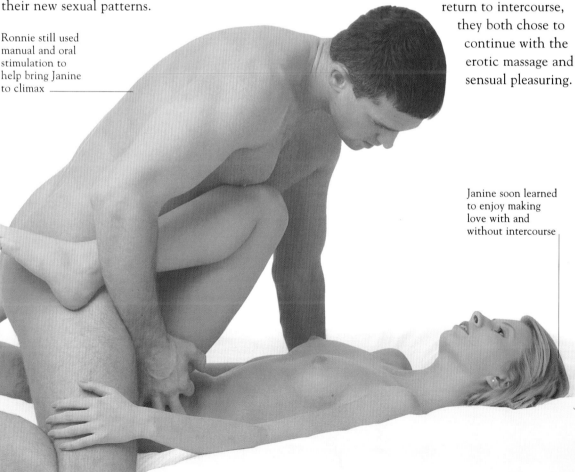

Janine soon learned
to enjoy making
love with and
without intercourse

DEALING WITH GRIEF

The normal components of grief—the shock, numbness, denial, and pain, the anger, guilt, and frustration, and the depression, exhaustion, and despair—will eventually go away, but it is vital that they be expressed. All too often, people feel that their grief should conform to a time limit and that to go over this limit is a weakness and an irritation to others. Suppressing your natural grieving process can actually extend your grief.

RECOVERING FROM BEREAVEMENT
Having someone with you who is caring and supportive as you work through the grieving process is very important. If that person is a lover, however, there may be difficulties if your grief imposes on your partner and your relationship.

Even if you feel that you are crying endlessly and your emotional state seems hopelessly out of control, rest assured that such open displays of grief do in fact help to bring you through your pain. You should never feel embarrassed by your grief, nor by anyone else's. Anyone who has suffered bereavement will understand your pain.

WORKING THROUGH THE STAGES OF GRIEF
It is generally accepted that the first stage of grief is characterized by shock, numbness, and disbelief. The sense of numbness can be frightening, but it soon passes. It is common for the bereaved person to be unwilling to accept what has happened. This can be disconcerting to friends, and especially to a partner who is also close to the bereaved.

THE PAIN OF LOSS
After the initial numbness has passed, there may be a period of intense emotional pain. In some cases this can manifest itself as physical pain, too. Many therapists feel that this is a very helpful and necessary part of the grieving process as the bereaved is unlikely to be able to accept the loss until he or she is able to vent the anguish.

DEALING WITH GUILT AND ANGER
The third stage of grieving often includes a period of intense anger and guilt. Often the anger will be directed at the deceased for abandoning those left behind, or at survivors (such as other family members), or at other people closely associated with the death—a doctor, for example.

Further anguish may be caused by the bereaved's sense of guilt. This may be caused by the need to justify the death of a loved one, to take on the blame, because otherwise the death cannot be justified. Other guilt may stem from unresolved arguments with the deceased, or the feeling that something had been left unsaid. There is a chance that the bereaved may alienate the very people he or she needs most at this time.

THE RECOVERY

The final stage of grieving can be the most difficult. Regaining the desire to enter social life again can be daunting. If the bereaved feels uncertain of emotional investment, or thinks that to enter a new relationship would be disloyal to the deceased, he or she may shy away from making new friends, or even socializing with old ones. Feelings of disloyalty and a lack of recent experience in dating can cause physical problems, too. Ronnie (*see pages 152–155*) found that the memory of his wife caused him to suffer sexual problems when he embarked on a new relationship.

If your partner is recently bereaved, it is important that you do not rush him or her into a confusing or vulnerable situation. Often the bereaved will need to take stock at every stage of the relationship, sometimes needing to move back a stage or two before feeling comfortable.

RECOVERY
You are over the worst when feelings of outrage and heartbreak are replaced by "ordinary" sadness. Rather than bursting into tears at the mention of the deceased, you will begin to enjoy reminiscing about the good times you shared, despite the fact that you are conscious of the loss.

DEALING WITH GRIEF

It can be upsetting to see your partner distressed and then to feel helpless about doing anything to relieve his or her pain. But rest assured that any support you offer will help greatly. Try not to feel pushed aside during your partner's grief. He or she may be too distressed to realize that you may also be grieving and in pain.

1 *If your partner is suffering from shock and denial it may be left to you to make the funeral arrangements. Involve your partner gently in the practical aspects of the funeral so that he or she may accept the fact of bereavement more easily.*

2 *If your partner is suffering from uncontrollable bouts of crying, insomnia, poor appetite, or weight loss, try to be as supportive as you can. Many people consider the funeral to be the end of a period of mourning, but such social and practical guidelines rarely have any effect on the emotional state of a person who is grieving.*

3 *If your partner experiences anger and guilt, he or she will need understanding and forgiveness, especially if the anger is unjustly directed at you. Try to encourage your partner to express his or her feelings, even if you then receive their rage.*

While your partner is working through this stage of bereavement, it is important that he or she is not left alone for too long. The aching and emptiness are much easier to bear if someone who cares is offering support and consolation.

INDEX

ADDITIONAL READING

ADLER, ALFRED
(translated Colin Brett)
Understanding Human Nature
Oneworld

ADLER, ALFRED
(translated Colin Brett)
What Life Could Mean to You
Oneworld

BARBACH, LONNIE G.
*For Each Other: Sharing
Sexual Intimacy*
Doubleday

CUTLER, WINNIFRED B.
Love Cycles: The Science of Intimacy
Random House

DINKMEYER, DON C., et. al.
*Adlerian Counselling
& Psychotherapy*
Macmillan

FRANCOEUR, ROBERT T. and
FRANCOEUR, ANNA K.
Becoming A Sexual Person
Macmillan

GRAY, JOHN
*Men Are From Mars, Women Are
From Venus: A Practical Guide For
Improving Communications & Getting
What You Want In Your Relationships*
HarperCollins

GRAY, JOHN
*Men, Women and Relationships:
Making Peace with the Opposite Sex*
Beyond Words

HOOPER, ANNE
Massage & Loving
Holt

HOOPER, ANNE
The Ultimate Sex Book
DK Publishing, Inc.

HOOPER, ANNE
Ultimate Sexual Touch
DK Publishing, Inc.

HYDE, JANET S.
Understanding Human Sexuality
McGraw Hill

ROWE, DOROTHY
*Depression: The Way
Out of the Prison*
Routledge

STOPPARD, MIRIAM
The Magic Of Sex
DK Publishing, Inc.

WILSON, BRADFORD and
EDINGTON, GEORGE
*First Child, Second Child: Your
Birth Order Profile*
Zebra

ACKNOWLEDGMENTS

Author's portrait: Jules Selmes
Photographic assistance: Neil Guegan
Hair and Makeup: Penny Attwood,
Andrea Black, Bettina Graham
Design assistance: Mercedes Morgan,
Carmel O'Neill, Karen Sawyer
Editorial assistance: Simon Warmer
Production consultant: Lorraine Baird